THE MUD-PIE DILEMMA

Timber Press Series in Arts and Crafts
Series Editor: Bridgett McCarthy, Director,
Portland Arts & Crafts Society

THE MUD-PIE DILEMMA

A Master Potter's Struggle
to Make Art and Ends Meet

John Nance

Timber Press
Forest Grove, Oregon

For Jason and T.R.

THE MUD-PIE DILEMMA
John Nance

© Copyright 1978 by Timber Press

Library of Congress catalog card number: 78-13888
ISBN: 0-917304-18-7

Timber Press
P.O. Box 92
Forest Grove, Oregon 97116

PREFACE

This book concerns four months in the life of a man, a potter, seeking to make art and seeking himself and his place in the world, in his family, in his work. In some ways he is all of us; in others he is unique—a particular man, in a particular place, in a particular time.

He has found that making art for a living means risking both the art and the livelihood, and that winning at one may mean losing at the other.

I do not want to make it sound too grand or too simple, but I do want to say these things at the start because while gathering the material I was surprised more than once to meet potters who were bothered by the book they thought I was doing. They expressed concern that potter Thomas Coleman was a bit young and yet-to-mature (although admittedly talented and able). They assured me I would be better off to observe and document a more widely recognized and mature master of the potting world.

But, as I tried to explain, this is not intended as a tribute to a venerated master, or a review of the potting life well spent, or the reflections of an arts/crafts sage. And although I have been interested in pottery for several years, I am not a potter, artist, craftsman, critic or connoisseur, so this is not a how-to book, a critique, or a survey of a period, style or region of potmaking.

This is a journalist's account of a man working at and for things he needs and loves. I often wished that I knew more, and understood better, certain things about the subjects and the context, but I also appreciated being comparatively free to inquire and observe without undue concern for "the right way" or "the right questions" of potmaking and the pottery world. Of course, this means experienced potters will find I have said too much about some things and too little about others, and laymen will find it vice-versa.

Among other difficulties was my belief that artworks speak best for themselves—that their very being is their statement—and that words about them risk being wrong, redundant and confusing.

Despite these pitfalls, I went ahead with this project because I was hooked on it, and because, otherwise, not as many people would see Coleman's work.

It was this latter probability that got the book started in the first place. Publisher Richard Abel has proclaimed that the Pacific Northwest of the United States harbors artists, scholars, and authorities in many fields who deserve to be known more widely. He proposed doing a series of short books about them and picked Coleman for the start. Abel knew of my interest in pottery and soon I was at work. The few months originally allotted to the project passed quickly, and now, one year later, the material is ready for the press.

My deepest thanks and appreciation go to Tom, Elaine, Jason and T.R. Coleman, in whose lives, household and studio I was always made to feel welcome.

Thanks must also be extended to many persons who are mentioned in the book. They are, however, too numerous to cite here and I hope the significance of their contributions is clear in the text and that my appreciation is known to each.

For reading the manuscript and making helpful and improving comments, I thank Tom and Elaine Coleman, Richard Abel, Patrick and Arthene Horsley, Elaine Andrews, Ruby Moll and Martha Jean Rutherford.

Deep gratitude goes to Robert Reynolds for his excellent help with graphics. The printing of black and white photographs was by Ritch Phillips in his shop, *Sometimes the Magic Works.*

And to my wife, Joyce, and children, Gillian and Christopher, I am grateful for the love and support that sustained me throughout.

CONTENTS

THE DILEMMA 1

THE STRUGGLE 3

THE SHOW 69

THE UNCERTAINTY 83

THE ART AND THE ENDS 109

"All the genuine, deep delight of life is in showing people the mud-pies you have made; and life is at its best when we confidingly recommend our mud-pies to each other's sympathetic consideration."
—J.M. Thorburn

"Art is a jealous mistress, and, if a man have genius for painting, poetry, music, architecture, or philosophy, he makes a bad husband and an ill-provider."
—Ralph Waldo Emerson

THE DILEMMA

On August 8, 1977, Thomas Coleman began making pottery for a show that was to open in Seattle, Washington on October 7. He expected to exhibit about 100 pieces—each one different and supposedly a work of art, which, depending on your definition of art, made the task either quite hard, excruciatingly difficult or virtually impossible.

Coleman himself tended to think of it as all three. So throughout July, while doing his regular production pottery and preparing material for the exhibit pieces, he worked himself physically and mentally up—like an athlete for a big game. He ran and meditated and studied every day. And he devised the time frame in which he was required to make all of the show pots in just eight weeks.

He could have started work on them earlier, but he wanted—felt he needed—to put himself under tight deadline pressure. "I have to go through this for every show anymore," he said, "each one seems to be harder than the last. Even though I want to do it, I dread it."

Thomas Coleman was 32 years old and had made his living as a potter for 11 years. He was married and had two children, talent, skill, ambition, a small bank account and a strong desire to make impressive pots and paint on them.

His stoneware was considered excellent (he spent about half his time working in stoneware), but porcelain was his specialty—and his obsession (all of the Seattle pots would be in porcelain). He was fond of throwing spectacularly large porcelains with ultra-thin walls. His decorations ranged from intricate designs to a single solid color, from soft greens and smokey blues to blood red.

Many knowledgeable judges believed Coleman was one of the best potters in the Pacific Northwest—perhaps in the entire United States. And some enthusiasts claimed he had no betters anywhere nowadays in the throwing and decorating of porcelain in the classical Chinese tradition.

While he was unknown on a national scale, his reputation had attained almost mythic proportions in some local circles. When I first heard of Coleman I asked a young woman who had been making pots in Oregon for several years if she knew him.

"No, I don't," she said, "but they say he is amazing. Would you believe that he throws porcelain this high (her hand patted air at waist level)? Porcelain! I mean that is like working in warm butter, right? A potter I know used to share a studio with him and told me that Coleman could be throwing a huge porcelain platter and be, say, two-thirds done and have to leave. Now get this. He would fold in the sides of the platter, cover it with a plastic sheet, and split. He'd come back later—next day even—remove the plastic, unfold the clay, and go right on throwing the platter! Like he'd never left. Hey, I mean that is outta sight. Almost weird, right? Got to be some kind of potter."

Not everyone was awed, of course, but even his critics expressed respect for his talent and expertise. It was notable also that two of the more sophisticated critics held opposing views—one contended Coleman's pottery was so refined and perfect that it lacked life; the other said it was so lush and unrestrained that it lacked discipline.

Coincidentally, as Coleman prepared for the Seattle exhibit, he was rankled by a newspaper review by the latter critic. It had appeared four months earlier, and concerned his last show, in Portland, which was extremely popular and had excellent sales. The reviewer's critical remarks were an exception which Coleman said did not bother him. In fact, though, he had been touched much more deeply than he was aware or would admit.

At least one other thing was bothering Coleman, but it had been for some time and was as old as art itself: How did a man give his best to the art he loved and to the family he loved too?

THE STRUGGLE

August 12, Canby—It was 103 degrees and Thomas Coleman stayed at the wheel all afternoon except to remove pots, fetch more clay, and make quick trips outside to drench himself with the garden hose.

Whooping and grinning, he dripped back into the studio after his third dousing and surveyed the room. The door, propped open in hope of catching a breeze, caught not a wisp. The studio was like a sauna. Coleman's curly hair stuck to his skin; water and sweat streamed down his face; his clothes were soaked.

"It's hot," he said, still grinning.

"You going to keep throwing?" I asked.

"Oh, yeah, guess so," he said. "We're started now. Better keep going."

He re-wedged a 20-pound ball of porcelain and plopped half of it on the wheel just as his two sons ran in. Jason, six, and T.R. (for Thomas Rae), four, stirred up clouds of grey-white dust as they chased one another and three dogs around the studio.

The dogs, which had either followed the boys in or were roused from napping under studio tables, were a small mongrel terrier named Tiller (short for (Rototiller); a larger rusty-red Irish Setter named Ruby (for Ruby Red), who with a loping stride and quick jaws could snap up thrown apples like a baseball shortstop; and a giant Doberman pinscher named Harley (from Harley-Davidson), who weighed well over 100 pounds, had ash-brown fur, pinkish eyes, and a gaping mouth spiked with pointed teeth.

"Harley's the only one you've got to worry much about," Coleman called out to me. "He sometimes just doesn't like somebody—bit a couple pretty bad—so go easy with him at the start. We can tie him up if we have to."

It was not long before the big Doberman came over to where I was taking photographs, stared at me and began to sniff. He apparently found the smell of my dog agreeable and pushed his muzzle into my ribs, nudging me off balance.

"Hey, that's good!" Coleman shouted. "He thinks you're okay. Wants you to scratch his head."

The boys, meanwhile, had taken up positions between drying racks and the throwing wheel, competing for their father's attention by teasing, pulling faces, making noises. Coleman, who by now had centered and opened his clay, finally stopped the wheel, gave the boys a stern stare and asked them to play outside. They pouted, but eventually left . . . and returned a few minutes later, giggling and scuffling, hurling bits of clay at one another. Coleman, showing patience a father who worked at home had to admire, glanced up a few times and told them to settle down. They didn't and he finally succeeded in moving them outside by threatening to cancel the river swim promised for later.

During these negotiations, which had been tricky at points, Coleman had worked sporadically on his pot, and also maintained the semblance of a conversation with me. The porcelain on the wheel had been pulled into a cylinder then shaped into a bowl that stood about 18 inches high. Children gone, he quickly finished it with a rib and some sponge-and-finger work, wire-cut it free of the wheel, lifted it with the tips of his fingers and put it beside other pots drying on a table.

He immediately grabbed another ball of clay, slapped it down and centered it—breaking off conversation for several seconds, his head making small circles in time with the spinning wheel. He resumed talking in mid-sentence and went silent again to open the pot. He then pulled the opened clay once—twice—three times up into a cylinder and began shaping it into a globe.

We chatted along again until Coleman, suddenly frowning and leaning closer to the wheel, seemed to shut out everything in the world except himself and the clay. His head dropped low and his cheek lay nearly against the whirling porcelain. His eyes narrowed, then widened, bulging out almost grotesquely and staring blankly into space as his fingers felt the way.

He was still more-or-less seated on his chair, but his whole body was tilted—one knee touched the floor and his torso bent sideways so far that his shoulders were almost perpendicular to the ground. His left shoulder was on top, upraised elbow pointing to the ceiling. His right hand reached down low, fingers on the pot's underbelly; his left hand worked inside.

"Hey, com'on," he said softly. "Com'on you . . . come on. Dammit! Careful, you sonuvabitch, be careful—damn you! . . . careful in there...haaa—so that's it; she's going, yep—but not yet. Oh no you don't, not yet you don't—Ha!"

Then, remembering me, he flicked his eyes up my way and said, "This is the hardest part—right now. This damned stuff is just about as thin as she'll go...everything gets a little tense for awhile...I...I'm pushing it...as far as I can...hold on...hold iiiiiit...."

The grey-white porcelain was wet and soft and sticky smooth in the sweltering heat. It gleamed as it spun, like a tiny planet. Coleman's wet face shone with light reflected from the clay. His breathing stopped while his hands rose together inside and outside the pot, then met at the rim for the last time. He exhaled loudly and blinked, eye-balls but a few inches from where his fingertips still played along the lip.

Straightening up, he scooted back his chair and looked. The pot glistened in the afternoon shadows, its curves and proportions in good form.

Coleman shook himself and relaxed. He waved toward a bakery rack that held several pots, each about three feet tall. "Having awfully bad luck with those," he said. That very morning he had discovered eight such pots cracked, ruined. "They're giving me hell. I've lost almost every large pot I've thrown."

"Hot weather have anything to do with it?"

"Maybe, but only a little. I think it's mostly something else. This happens a lot when you stretch porcelain this thin and large...there's so much tension. Of course the heat doesn't help, though, and if I don't get this cracking stopped there won't be any show at Seattle. This could get upsetting."

He glanced at the wall clock and decided to throw one more piece before quitting. Quickly making a tall cylinder, he began shaping it into a bowl. When the mouth was about 10 inches wide (the body about 16 inches high) the walls looked about one quarter of an inch thick at the middle and perhaps twice that at the base and rim.

Coleman started reducing the upper thickness. His right hand seemed to float on the outside, tips of index finger and thumb grazing the clay while the other fingers occasionally squeezed a palmed sponge. This released streaks of water that widened into dark bands as they encircled the bowl. Coleman's left hand was completing a pass inside when an overhead light dimmed for a moment...an electric power fluctuation. The wheel twitched, the thin wall of clay wavered—possibly snagging on a fingertip or knuckle—and produced two barely perceptible slumps, first in the bowl and then in Coleman's shoulders.

"Dammit!" he yelled and sat silent. After more curses, he horse-laughed and slapped the crippled pot flat and then into a mound.

The end had come so swiftly that I hardly realized what had happened. Staring down at the remains I was impressed by the suddenness with which a lively and splendid bowl had disappeared. Vague curves and planes of the pot-that-was were visible in the grey wreckage. There was something vibrant and attractive about that mass of smashed clay; I felt an unexpected urge to plunge my hands into it, but did not, and the moment passed.

Coleman peeled the lump from the bat and plopped it into a barrel. "Screw it," he said with a shrug, "let's get out of here. Time for a swim."

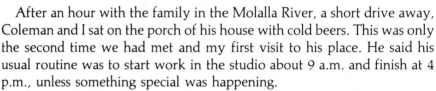

After an hour with the family in the Molalla River, a short drive away, Coleman and I sat on the porch of his house with cold beers. This was only the second time we had met and my first visit to his place. He said his usual routine was to start work in the studio about 9 a.m. and finish at 4 p.m., unless something special was happening.

I asked if he took regular vacations or did much traveling.

"Travel? Oh, man, would I love to travel," he said. "I really want to, I need to, but I haven't had the chance. I've hardly traveled anywhere in my whole life. And it has been about three years since we've had a vacation—oh, we had a day off here and there, but no real time off. It's always just one thing after another—finish a show, get home and start throwing the good old bread-and-butter production stuff, then another show, and then it's time to start producing for Christmas . . . or something. It never stops."

This included a growing participation by Tom's wife, Elaine. The quality and quantity of her pots had improved steadily as the boys took less of her time. She had given up her art studies when they got married, to work and help pay Tom's way through school, and resumed potting on a small scale in the mid-'70s.

I learned later that the Colemans had been grossing about $30,000 a year the last few years. After expenses (mainly the 25 to 50 per cent paid to sales agents), the net dropped to between $9,000 and $16,000 annually.

After taxes, living expenses took it all. They had done considerably better than that one year, Tom said, "But it was a killer. We were on the go *constantly*—shows, fairs, galleries—and it just wasn't worth it—took everything out of me, drained me. I decided I just couldn't work that hard simply for money."

That may have been partly responsible for a serious decline in Tom's health. He had been treated off and on since childhood for allergies, asthma and hypertension, and making pottery aggravated those problems. It also led to a bad back. The years of mixing and throwing clay and handling the large pots took him to a point in 1974 when seating himself at the wheel required a full minute of slow and painful movements. Doctors recommended an operation. It laid Coleman up for three weeks and cost $5,000 (mostly covered by insurance), but improved his back. The doctors warned, however, that continued strain and stress could revive the problem.

I did not know all these things that first time we sat on the porch, but the difficulty of this kind of life was already clear. I asked Coleman if he had ever considered another kind of career.

"No, not really," he said. "I know I complain about all this, but it's what I do. I like it—like pots, like making them—as corny as that sounds. Also—and this surprises some potters—I even like the social junk that goes with it, the sales and politicking and game-playing—you know, the competition and psyching each other out, the show openings and all that BS. It takes a lot out of you, but it's part of it. Elaine can't stand that stuff, but it gives me a kick. . . ."

That sounded positive and I asked him if this enabled him to usually make the kind of pots he wanted, that satisfied him.

"What? I didn't say that."

But wasn't this what he was ultimately seeking, to make things that gave him fulfillment? I said.

"Oh sure—I'd love to make some pots just for myself. Now these I'm making will be good, but to make things strictly for me, well, hell, now *that* would really be something. But hardly anybody gets to do that."

What would he make?

"I don't know. I'd take a year at least, like a sabbatical. No telling what I'd do—test myself, I imagine, try some new things. I do some of that now, but I make only small discoveries, important just to me, like how far to push this clay or what that glaze will do. Sure I'd love to have a year without shows and sales and all the stuff that pays the bills."

He paused, then added, "I don't mean that our functional stuff isn't good—it is—but I've done all that for years, over and over and over. I can do some of that stuff and watch TV at the same time. It's true, I do."

So why not do more experimental work?

"I've tried, but you've got to be free and loose. You need lots of time to just experiment and play around. We've got too many bills for that. But what the hell, it's not just me that has that problem—look at the really great potters, people I've had as heroes; I've gotten to know some of them and it's also hard for them to keep growing. Take Voulkas, for instance—a giant, a great person—but even he says he's been doing the same stuff for years . . . ."

Coleman shook his head, shrugged, and sighed. "You've got to grow, but it's so hard to keep going," he said. "I want to . . . but you get stuck and keep doing the things that keep you eating."

He seemed a bit down, depressed, but seconds later clapped his hands together and said he had better get ready to go running. He usually covered about five miles, he said, and hated it, but did it to burn off nervous energy so he could relax at the end of the day, and because Elaine was Italian and cooked lots of pastas and rich foods.

"I love that stuff, I'd be a blimp if I didn't exercise every day," Coleman said. "I've got to run to keep my weight down."

This was hard to believe. He was about six feet tall and weighed no more than 150 pounds, slim as a dancer. I said it was impossible to imagine him fat.

"Oh sure, it's really bad," he insisted. "I have to watch the old calories all the time." There was no smile; he was serious.

Driving home shortly after that, the idea of him running to keep slim caused me to think more deeply about misleading appearances. In our first meeting, which was to discuss the possibility of my documenting his work, Coleman had been intelligent, amiable and very sensible. I was aware of that, but it was not the main impression I brought away although I had not realized this until now. Coleman's blue eyes, curly golden-brown hair and well-shaped facial features all came together on a pale smooth skin that was almost beardless.

The dominant impression was of buoyancy and freshness—youth. Despite whatever maturity or wisdom Coleman may have shown, that image of handsome boyishness was so visually strong that it automatically came to mind when I thought of Coleman. But now, after having seen him at work only one day, having seen his pots take form and having come in contact with the intensity and complexity of his personality, the image broadened, was vastly more interesting.

Included in that was a quick something of mind or spirit that sparked within Coleman and would be hard to grasp. It had flickered several times today, in slightly wild shouts when the work went good, in a surge of intense energy when he was challenged, in a sudden angry glint that flashed in his eyes when a thing went bad.

August 14, Canby—It was blistering hot again as I drove toward the Colemans' studio in the early afternoon. Heat vapors shimmered up from the six-lane asphalt highway taking me out of Portland toward Canby, where the Colemans lived and worked on a renovated farm.

For 10 miles the roadside was lined by used-car lots, motels, service stations, fast-food outlets and so forth. Then, just beyond Oregon City, the highway narrowed to two lanes and dropped down beside the Willamette River. Rocky cliffs and water, fields of grass and trees spread in all directions. The change was so swift and thorough it was startling. After a few miles, a turnoff took me past truck farms, nut orchards, and small ranches to a dusty driveway marked by a formal and imposing wooden sign on a post. Hand-carved Old-English script said, "Thomas L. Coleman."

Turning in, high yellow grasses speckled with flowers laced a barbed wire fence bordering the driveway. The road ran back through two or three acres of flatland, some freshly plowed and some green with garden. Near the center, tall trees shaded a tidy two-story farmhouse. The front porch faced a yard of freshly mowed grass decorated by, among other things, a rock pond with lily pads and an overturned tricycle.

The driveway went alongside the house and crossed behind it, past a pile of firewood and a rusty red pickup truck and a rickety tractor shed. A large stained glass window looked out of the house's rear wall, next to a screened porch. Opposite them was a small grove of apple trees. The road passed between the house and the trees and at the grove's end turned sharply right and continued about 100 feet to the front door of the Colemans' studio.

The studio joined and added to what had been three wooden structures on the old farm—a small, peaked-roof barn; a stable; and a poultry coop-workshop. The barn stood in the center with the stable and coop extending on opposite sides like wings. On the front of all hung coils of rusty wire, farm tools, ceramic platters, bowls, and jugs at irregular intervals. And at the rear east corner stood a shiny new sheet metal shed.

Coleman was visible through the open front door of the former poultry coop and waved me inside. This was now the main workroom, where pottery was thrown, built, biscuit-fired and decorated. It was squarish, about 20'×25'. Three walls had tall, Roman-arch windows that had come from a razed hospital. The fourth wall was against the side of the barn and was covered with photographs, posters, prints, drawings, old calendars and advertisements. Elaine's work tables were along the opposite wall and Tom's one-horsepower Alpine potting wheel was near the open front door, beside one of the tall windows.

A door in the rear led to a room used for drying, glazing, storing and firing pots. It had a 12-cubic-foot downdraft kiln, wide skylights, and rows of barrels, shelves and mobile bakery racks. A door on the south end led to the sheet metal sheds which housed a newly built, propane-fired, 75-cubic-foot Minnesota Flattop kiln. A door at the other end led into the old barn. It had only one room and was used for storage and packing, but had been intended for display and sales, with banks of overhead floodlights, tiers of shelves and a pot-bellied stove.

You had to go back outside to enter the north wing (the old stable) where supplies were stored and clay mixed in a five HP U.S. Navy surplus dough-mixing machine. Partitioned areas contained old furniture, rusty farm equipment, and a Harley-Davidson motorcycle. The big bike sat in a stable strewn with straw; dust dimmed the black leather and silver chrome. When Coleman showed me around he paused here and gazed at the machine. "That was a fine bike," he said. "Had her for years but don't ride anymore—even if I had the time, my back wouldn't let me."

A place of their own—a home and studio—was important to both Tom and Elaine, each of whose childhoods had been upset by the difficulties and divorces of their parents. Tom, an only child, was born in Amarillo, Texas (February 16, 1945), and moved as his father bought and/or managed hotels in Oklahoma, California, Washington and Oregon. Home, then, was a series of hotel rooms until his parents divorced and nine-year-old Tom went to live with his maternal grandmother in suburban Portland. He would later spend time with both parents, but his grandmother's house remained home until he was 19, had graduated from high school, and was enrolled in the Portland Art Museum School.

He majored in drawing and painting, intending to become a "fine artist." After two years, Coleman believed he was on the right track, but earning a living looked awfully far away—and he wanted to marry Elaine Klock, a fellow student at the art school. Tom had taken a course in pottery, which he enjoyed and which promised quicker and more certain financial returns than painting, so he switched his major to ceramics, married Elaine, and in 1968 completed a thesis on glaze formulations and graduated with a B.A. degree.

Following an apprenticeship-of-sorts with Bill Creitz, who was the hottest potter around Oregon in those days, Coleman got started selling his own production ware at art fairs and craft shows, while teaching pottery on the side to make enough to live.

Coleman's work and sales grew, and so did his family. The Colemans moved from apartments to a house, and then to a larger house. These were fine except burglars hit them three times in the early 1970s. With that, plus the need for more spacious studio facilities, and an urge to give rural living a try, they found an old farm at Canby, not too far from the community of Lake Oswego where Elaine had gone to high school.

It took a lot of work to make an acceptable studio and refurbish the house and add a large room—the main structures had been built in the 1890s—but things steadily became more comfortable and attractive and efficient. There were some drawbacks, of course, such as the 25-mile drive into Portland and the high pollen content of farm country, which played havoc with Tom's hay fever and meant Elaine had to mow the huge lawn.

Coleman talked about these things as he worked and later as we sat on the porch, relaxing with beers on my second visit to the studio. I inquired also about the development of his career after he graduated from the museum school.

Coleman said Bill Creitz had been an important figure, not only for the inspiration of his pot making but also because he was tough. "He came around one afternoon, looked at my pots and said they were junk," Coleman recalled. "He said they were just copies of his stuff—and then he busted them, *smashed* them all! I was devastated—but it made a huge difference in my work. I had to learn my own way; Creitz made me. And there was no quick way."

Coleman was speaking casually but with seriousness. "You've got to go through all the phases, no shortcuts. There's no way you can be a potter if you try and skip, say, the production part of it. And you cannot avoid drudgery either. Here's an example. Since I started making pots I've tried all kinds of things and I've always had to overcome bad clay to do it. All my clay in my early years was horrible, awful—but I didn't know that at the time. And when I did figure it out, I didn't know what to do about it. I finally realized I had to mix my own. Now I mix it all. In fact, I've never bought a completely satisfactory ready-mixed clay. My stoneware has 18 different ingredients—that's a lot, I know, but it's worth it because with that number a couple of defective ingredients won't ruin the whole batch. My porcelain costs about 30 cents a pound and I have to get all the materials from England. The British silicas are excellent, and my grolleg China clay comes from there; their kaolin is also very fine. Frankly, only the British do justice to raw materials strictly for potters. Big manufacturers here in the States can't be bothered with the relatively small volume bought by potters. So you've got to look around, and the English give us a break." He added that his favorite authority on porcelain was John Reeves, a Britisher who had conducted hundreds of experiments and led Tom to the grolleg-based formula Tom considered his best.

Sketching in some of his development, he said that he had started making simple stoneware pots and by 1969 they were getting more complicated—"sometimes it would take me three or four hours to set up, and I'd paint eyeglasses on them, or stripes." By 1971 he had been influenced by Japanese and Korean potters; his decorations included animals, ming trees, washes, and he started making yo-yo boxes. In 1972 he worked heavily in salt glazes—"and my decorations got very busy. I had a real problem learning to stop decorating, to leave things alone. That has continued to be difficult for me." In 1973 he got into black on rutile slip and was continuing to work with stoneware, but it had been disappointing him for some time.

The main problem was that he had not been able to paint on stoneware as he wished, and painting had been his strongest artistic point. Searching for more suitable material, he experimented with porcelain—and was hooked. It provided a smooth white surface on which to paint, and, furthermore, had plastic and tactile properties that were exciting. Before long potting began to rival painting as the most important force in his work. Coleman spent all of his available time experimenting with porcelain formulas, glazes, decorations and techniques that would give him the best combinations.

"The potters who influenced me most right then were Bill Creitz, Bob Sperry and Jerry Glenn—all working in stoneware. In porcelain there was nobody around, so I just went ahead on my own. One of the most important things I learned is that you have to give porcelain total consciousness, you must constantly be concerned with form—even with the simplest shape you can think of—because if it's not right, it's bad. It *must* be right because mistakes show up so clearly in porcelain, there is no funkiness, no roughness to hide behind. So you pay constant attention, actually struggle with the clay. You have to use force with ease, if you know what I mean—force it gently."

He had been exhibiting his work since 1969—producing at least two or three one-man shows each year—and in the early 1970's the porcelains began to dominate them. But porcelains took much more time and energy to make, which meant he had to raise his prices, which in turn meant he had to go through the better galleries and shops. The pots got larger, the prices got larger, and so did his reputation.

"But even now," he said, "while porcelain is my major work, I can't leave stoneware alone for more than three or four months. After porcelain it is so relaxing, a joy, so smooth and flowing—I always go to stoneware for that quality. Porcelain is so difficult—always challenging you, so rigorous and tense...but, of course, the pleasure of opening a kiln with porcelain inside is something *fantastic*."

It was a warm evening, so we had more beer and kept talking. I asked if teaching offered a satisfactory answer to the problems of making pots and a living, too.

"I once thought it might," he said. "I taught steadily at various places for about eight years, and I liked it a lot at the start. I learned some things and helped some people, but it got awfully tiresome. And later on the students didn't have any patience—they wanted to go faster with everything. Give a throwing demonstration and they'd groan if they thought you took too long with a piece. You couldn't show them the right way, they just wanted to get on the wheels and *get going*."

Coleman said he had been teaching at Portland State University when the market for pots took a sudden huge rise. "Wow, when the word got around that they could learn to throw in a few months and go right out and make some money, the students just poured in. Most of their pots were barely passable, but they still sold."

He laughed and shook his head, remarking that when he had begun potting a dozen years ago there were probably only 15 or 20 persons making pots for a living in the whole state—and now there were probably 2,000 trying to make all or part of their living producing pots.

I expressed disbelief and he insisted that the 2,000 figure was probably even low—"I don't know exactly, of course, but 2,000 is not too many. Look at all the schools turning people out." (I subsequently mentioned those figures to many potters, school directors and teachers, gallery owners and managers—and none had more precise figures, but all said that Coleman's sounded about right.)

There was some good in the boom, Coleman added, but more bad. "The school took advantage—the classes brought in good income, helped pay for other things in the art department—and we just cranked out the students. So everyone was guilty—the kids for wanting the fast bucks, the school for jumping on the bandwagon, and me for teaching it. Eventually I got as depressed as I was bored. I had to stop."

I suggested that all those students must have expanded the market; surely not all would keep potting, and they would have developed an appreciation for pots and become buyers.

That was probably true to a degree, Coleman said, but the sad fact was that some of the best young potters failed financially while second-rate craftsmen did well.

"Some people just can't, or won't, sell their stuff," he said. "And nobody ever teaches you in school that you have *got* to sell those pots. There's no choice for most of us—sell or forget it. And it is so damned frustrating to know that excellent pots can sit in studios gathering dust while the potters, who want to sell them, just grit their teeth and watch totally stupid pots bring in the cash."

If it was so hard to make a living, then, why did so many people keep coming into the field?

Tom reckoned that there continued to be a market and that making mediocre pots was easy—or at least not hard. It did not take exceptional talent or exhaustive work and the life style was fashionable and looked good: "It's laid back, man," he said. "That's what it is these days, *laid back*, yessir. And it's possible to make it as a production potter for a long time; some make a good steady income."

Why was it, then, that he had mentioned so often the problems of making a living?

"Oh, well, if I would just make straight production pots, sure I'll make a decent living—and I'll also go crazy. I can work at it two or three months at a crack, but then it starts to bore me to death. I can only make so many hundred of something and then I start to crack. Maybe that's one reason why I love porcelain—you can't do production with it."

Just before I left the farm, I brought up a newspaper review which I had overheard him discussing the first day we met. (I learned later that the review criticized a Coleman exhibit that generally won praise, had sold 70 of 96 pots displayed, and grossed roughly $7,000.) The review obviously had bothered him and I asked why.

"Naw, I didn't really mind the review so much," he said with a slight frown pulling his eyebrows together. "What got me was all these potters I've known for years using it as a springboard to jump all over me. Now *that* was depressing. No, what the review said didn't bother me, it was the people who'd call up or send a letter and refer to the review as some way to come down on me. That hurt."

It looked as if it was hurting him now. The frown had deepened and his eyes narrowed. Mouth corners tightened and made a downward slash.

"Why didn't they have the guts to tell me that stuff before?" he went on. "They'd always say things like, 'Hey, man, I dig your stuff,' or 'Great show, man,' or 'I really like this or that.' But, hell, it turned out that some of 'em didn't like it at all—been putting me on for years! I wouldn't do that—I wouldn't tell somebody I liked their stuff if I didn't."

August 17, Canby—The extraordinary heat wave was in its tenth day. Each one had reached between 95 and 103 degrees, and before this day was out it would hit 105. The studio air was damp and heavy when I walked in. Coleman sat at the wheel, dripping. He looked tired. Dark crescents underlined his eyes and his whole face had a pinched look, as if he had a headache or tasted something sour. Working with the clay, he lacked his usual graceful smoothness; his moves were forced.

We exchanged but a few words. After he finished the piece he was working on, he switched off the wheel and jerked his head toward a table full of bisqued pots. "More cracks!" he said loudly. "Had to throw out a big bunch of pieces yesterday, and more today. Dammit, if this keeps up we'll have to cancel Seattle. Hate to do that. I rarely cancel. There was a time I simply would not do it, never, no matter what. But I'm not so up-tight about that anymore . . . sometimes it just takes too much out of you to make it; not worth it." He shook his head several times.

The hot weather was making difficult problems worse, he said. Extreme heat created textural and consistency problems because the surface clay dried too fast, developed a trace of crustiness even as he was throwing it. Coleman said he thought this might contribute to the cracking.

"Aw, but I don't know," he grumbled, "got to figure this out, or . . . dammit! You know, even when I say it's better not to do a show than knock yourself out, I still feel it is very important to make it on time. I *want* to make it . . . ."

Just then Jason and T.R. came screeching down a path and chased one of the dogs into the studio.

"Awright! Awright! Now don't get started with that in here now!" Coleman commanded. "Out! I mean it, com'on, let's go. Everybody *out*. You too, Harley. I got too much work today. We'll swim later, okay? Now leave us alone. Com'on. Goodbye. Out! Out! Out!"

They straggled out and Coleman shut the door. He walked to the table of drying pots, overturned one and pointed to a place on the base, next to his signature. Leaning down, I saw a hairline about one-inch long. The mark was hardly noticeable.

"Is this what you're talking about," I said. "That's all? That's a crack?"

"Right."

"But you can hardly see it. It doesn't even go all the way through the clay. Can't it be repaired or filled or something?"

"Oh no, you can't do that . . . I mean, you *can* do it but you mustn't. No-no, that's no good. The piece is cracked and that's that. Some potters might overlook it—put 'em out that way or patch 'em, but we never do that. A pot is right or it's not. You can't have it both ways. Once you've got a reputation for making a certain kind of pot, you've got to stick to it."

He said he had discarded eight of every 10 large pieces he had thrown in the past week because they had cracked on the drying table or in the bisque kiln. Many hours of work were lost.

"It's the combination of shrinkage, this heat, and the goddam porcelain," Coleman said harshly. "I don't know, I've been thinking of trying some grog, but I hate to put it into the clay, especially since it's porcelain."

He went to the wheel and resumed throwing a bowl, continuing a flow of words except when, as before, a piece demanded his full concentration. Asked about his talking, Coleman gave a snorting laugh.

"I must drive just about everybody crazy that I work with," he said. "I used to share a studio with a couple of real good guys—Pat Horsley and Don Sprague—and I must have driven 'em nuts. I can't help it, I just talk. Got to, I guess. Talk to myself all the time. I mean, what the hell, why not? Besides, I'm so wired that I've got to talk or do something—if I didn't then I'd go crazy . . . same reason why I run every night. Got to wind down. Ha! But then in the morning it takes me a couple of hours after I wake up to come in here and start work. Oh yeah, I'm really bad in the mornings. Sometimes a loud noise or the kids yelling or just being touched can blow me away. It's bad. I spend a couple of hours getting settled down so I can work. Every morning is like that. But once I get going it's fine; I swing along and it feels good. I like it, enjoy it. But getting started—tough, harder all the time."

A phone on the wall next to the front door rang and then stopped—Elaine answered it in the house. Seconds later her faintly heard shout told Tom to take it.

"Okay, whatta *you* want?" he said in a mock bellow, smiling. The caller apparently responded in kind and Coleman laughed and spent several minutes exchanging potting gossip and hassling. The handpiece of the phone was coated white with dried clay, and later I asked Tom if he always took calls—I had known craftsmen who refused when working. Tom said he almost always took them.

His studio had a constant buzz of sound—from him, the wheel, the bisque kiln, the children, the dogs, the phone, the twin-speaker radio. The radio was usually tuned to an FM station that maintained a steady flow of folk, jazz, and rock music. But when an announcer came on, even though Coleman was in conversation, he seemed to hear every word. Today, as he did everyday, while throwing a pot, he interrupted his own talking to shout comments at the radio. He then hummed a ditty, followed by a rhyme that had nothing to do with the radio, the conversation preceding it, or anything else immediately apparent.

Before I could make suitable response, Coleman, whose tired look was now completely gone, shook his head and said he was sick of gossipy potters who kept complaining about a fair he was in this summer. It seemed that he and his potter friend Tom Tibbs and their wives had made pots together and taken them to Bellevue, Washington's annual summer crafts' fair. The pots sold fairly well, and Coleman later received phone calls saying that a certain potter had been counting on that fair to cover his house payments, but instead did very poorly because the Coleman-Tibbs' pots took away a lot of his expected sales.

"I don't know if that's true—have no idea," Tom said. "How were we supposed to know he figured to make his whole nut on this one fair? They claim now that he *always* made it at Bellevue and now he's wiped out—made only $600 up there, had expected several thousand. So what am I supposed to do?"

The Tibbses and Colemans together had grossed about $4,000, he said, but expenses took most of that and the venture overall was not a great success. They had experimented with a line of stoneware dinnerware using all the mechanical devices they could find to increase production volume and cut costs. It was not bad pottery, but not so good either. Tom was quick to mention that he did not put his name on the pieces, which were signed only "OPW" for Oregon Potters Workshop.

As long as we were on annoying subjects, I mentioned that I had not been able to find a copy of the offending review of his last show and asked for more details.

Coleman said he could not remember exactly, but that the reviewer—a young woman named Susanna Kuo, an artist herself—had picked out some things in the exhibit as being fine art, then sort of lumped all the rest as flashy, show-off porcelains which merely displayed his technical abilities and had no merit as art. "Well, okay, all right!" he exclaimed with heat. "Some of it wasn't supposed to be art. That's right. I always have to make a bunch that will sell—and I know which ones those will be. And sure enough, they sold right out. But that's what it is all about too. If you don't sell something then where are you?" He made a helpless shrug, then added, "What got me most was all the phone calls from other potters.

More came after the Bellevue thing and the combination was too much. At the same time, some people down at Contemporary Crafts (the gallery where the Portland show was held) heard about the pots I had done for Bellevue and warned me to not do that anymore because it hurt my reputation as an artist. So what are you supposed to do? You're always going to upset somebody. And I've got bills—doctors', insurance, mortgage, maybe just the old food bills—you've got to make some money. Is that so damned bad?"

The more he talked the more vigorous, even cheerful, he seemed to become. And despite the intense heat he had continued working steadily on some very large jars.

"Anyway," he continued, "Susanna is very bright, a very good critic and writer. Although I don't know her I wanted to talk to her about that review but never have. I had read several of her reviews before and always agreed with her—sure, I was usually with her right down the line. I'd see a show and then read her review and we had almost the same opinions. So, when she takes me apart I've got to think about it, right?"

"Does that mean she was correct?"

"Well, maybe...at least about some things. I don't know. I'm still thinking about it."

"Will it influence your work, change it?"

"Change it? Oh, no! No way! I'm doing the same kind of things for the Seattle show. What she doesn't know is that I always do certain things—even though I do a lot of new pots—probably too many—I realize that, I always have too many; I'm willing to take some out but when we set up the show nobody wants to. Anyway, I always like to make a piece for each different period of my work—you know, one piece like I was doing in the late sixties, another for this style, and another for that. I like to keep a hand in each period. It's a reminder of where I've been, that I haven't forgotten, that I can still do it—still work in that style. It's fun, I enjoy it."

I asked if all the work for a show was worth it.

"Absolutely. You go around and get feedback; it helps you find out where you are, how you're doing. Not so much from other potters, but from the plain people. They talk about this piece or that one. And they are buying, so they like it or they don't, and they tell you one way or another. I need that now and then. Of course, this doesn't mean you know exactly where you stand, but it helps tell if you are getting across what you intended, whether they understand—or even care—what you are trying to do. I think a lot do, and that's important to me."

He finished a large jar and carried it to a table, which, together with a large five-shelved bakery rack, was filled with pots, some green, some bisque-fired. In the late afternoon sunlight the shapes looked golden. There were small round bottles, boxes and bowls, tall jars, urns and vases. The smoothness of their surfaces invited touching. . .and my hand slipped easily over the porcelain, finding it surprisingly warm and textured despite the appearance of creamy coolness. These pots had a beauty I had not anticipated. They had a simple purity, and at this moment, I said, I liked them better than decorated and fired pots.

"Sure, that's true," Tom said, who had walked over beside me. "Sometimes I'd like to leave 'em all this way." He smiled and put his arms around a ginger jar and gave it a hug.

"But," he added, "as much as I like them at this stage, I have got to say that form is not my big thing. I'm most interested in decorating, painting. You could say that I'm really just making a different kind of surface to paint on—a kind of round canvas. Glazing is boring to me, but painting—decorating—is exciting. I started as a painter, and I was a pretty good draftsman at one time. Of course the throwing was plenty rewarding and exciting to me when I was getting started; now, I don't know. . .I find that I have to throw a shape at least 200 times before I'm really comfortable with it, really good at it. Then, if I decide to keep it, it should feel like mine."

I asked what was the hardest thing for him to make.

"Teapot. It uses all your skills; really shows what you can do. All the parts are different and have to come together. And they all have to work or the pot fails."

Did he think of himself as an artist or craftsman, or both, or was that simply a trite question?

"It's hard to answer. As a craftsman, I guess I make some things chiefly to earn a living, but that doesn't mean I stint on quality, though I do hold back on artistic input. Every single piece cannot be a work of art—there are too many pieces. Yet every piece must be as true a piece of craftsmanship as I can make it—no seconds; we never put out seconds. If a piece isn't technically as good as we can do, then we bust it, nail it on the barn wall, or feed the dogs out of it."

It was far past his usual quitting time and Coleman was soaked with sweat and grimy, but he was in much better spirits than a few hours ago. Somewhere along the way he had found himself a friendly groove and worked—or maybe talked—his way into it. The stiffness was gone and he again had that effortless grace with the clay. It was a pleasure.

Emotional ups and downs seemed to be an accepted part of Coleman's existence as I watched him at work that autumn. He never let these fluctuations halt his work, however, and had techniques for dealing with them. Elaine, of course, did also. I suspected that words and noise, language and other sounds, were used by him—possibly subconsciously—to help adjust his flow of energy or to tune his moods and emotional rhythms to his work. Talking and mumbling and yelling released pressure, heightened enthusiasm, maintained production, paced concentration. And words were sometimes a cover, a mask or protection that helped him stay loose and on course.

Verbal games got silly and absurd as we spent more time together. Each of us was fond of jokes and stories in dialect, no matter how ineptly we did them, and the studio was often in an uproar. It would have been nonsensical prattle to anyone hearing it later, but it was gut-busting hilarity when you were there, sharing in the byplay of tensions and releases, laughing your head off. And, of course, sometimes it was just plain fun, enjoying the hell out of whatever, being alive, having the moment. It was, at those times, a rare playfulness.

And there were times when his seriousness, his respect for potmaking, or his stubbornness or pride pushed him on. Many weeks later I was to see Coleman seemingly near exhaustion. He had been working long hours for many days, had experienced some professional disappointments, and was having asthma and/or allergy attacks combined with incipient bronchitis that left him so congested and hoarse that his voice was a raspy croak. And he was scheduled to put on a slide show that evening for about 40 potters and students and a six-hour demonstration workshop the next day.

I felt certain that he would not be able to do it, but he apparently never considered that. He took medication all day as he sorted and arranged hundreds of slides. At the appointed hour he went to the gallery, set up his projector, introduced himself to the audience, "Hello, how are you? I'm Tom Coleman, could we have the lights out, please," and began the show. His voice was fuzzy but fully audible and he talked virtually nonstop for about 90 minutes.

The next morning he had a sore throat, running nose, puffy eyes, and foghorn voice. He said he was always like this in the morning and wedged his porcelain clay while waiting for the group to assemble.

At about 8:30 A.M. he arranged his material and tools on a table beside a throwing wheel and sat down to make pots. He accompanied this with sort of casual running commentary about his dealings with porcelain, how he defined it, what it should do. He made no mention of having a cold or not feeling well, and as the workshop got going his voice seemed to gain strength, his eyes brightened. He finished one bowl and worked up a teapot, then speaking with increasing enthusiasm, he demonstrated his method of centering.

Questions came from the audience on throwing rings and making sinks and the mixing of porcelain. Another person asked about stoneware and he said it gave him relaxation—"I listen to music as I throw—to flow and feel it form, it's so smooth. . . ."

While talking, he threw a half dozen more pieces—a bowl, two vases, a platter, a goblet, and a large upside-down form to demonstrate an easier way to throw a difficult flat-topped piece. Everything looked easy, but most persons in the room were professionals and recognized the skill involved. Murmurs of talk attended this or that bit of handiwork, and when he sliced through a tall cylinder to show the extreme thinness of the walls there was a communal gasp.

He did not, however, make a showy dramatic presentation and almost meandered along from one piece to the next, interspersing explanations with anecdotes, answers to questions, jokes. Beautifully formed pots kept spinning up out of his hands as he talked on throwing techniques, formulas, kilns, pottery schools, apprenticing ("the best way to learn—but hard to make work"), making a living, and the miseries of potting ("Clay dust is rotten for your lungs, same for the sprays and silica. Just about everything a potter does is bad for him: lifting bags of clay—and breathing the wet clay, that's carcinogenous stuff—but what the hell, we go on. I just don't think about it.").

After a break for lunch, he demonstrated trimming, brushwork, sprays, and a wide range of decorating techniques. By 4 p.m., seven-and-one-half hours after he began, Coleman's energy was obviously flowing strong and his voice was louder and clearer than any time all day. He finished the demonstrations, but questions kept him going until nearly 6 p.m. During a break, while waiting for Tom to disengage from several potters, Elaine told about a show she and Tom had put on a few years ago at Walla Walla, Washington.

"We had been invited to exhibit at this gallery and went all out," she said. "Flyers were sent early. Tom and I arrived a day ahead to set up everything just right. The people who owned the place were nice and helpful, and we got the pots arranged, refreshments all spread out. . .and three people came. Three. We sat around and talked to each other and drank the punch and ate the food. Three people the whole day!"

Was everybody upset?

"No, it was okay; oh, the gallery people were a little embarrassed, but we left some pots and they eventually sold them all and asked for more. They did fine."

I asked if Tom was bothered by the tiny turnout and Elaine said, "No, he wasn't upset at all. In fact, he really seemed to have a good time, just talked and looked around town all day . . . ."

August 27, Canby—Coleman was at work when I arrived, clay streaking his cheeks like warpaint and an old blue baseball cap pushing his hair out in fuzzy puffs around his ears. It was late morning, the heat wave had finally broken, and the studio was just pleasantly warm.

Tom seemed in a good mood. I had been unable to come to the farm for more than a week and in the same breath he said hello he observed that it must be nice to work just one day out of 10. Jason and T.R. dashed in and out again, giggling and bumping, and he persuaded them to go outside and stay awhile. Then he pushed his baseball cap back on his head, folded his arms across his chest, and grinned. The news, he said, was very good—he had found a way to stop large pots from cracking.

He explained that putting grog into the clay when it was being mixed gave the clay body more tensile strength. He had tried various grogs in the past and none were satisfactory—they did not combine properly with porcelain clay, shrunk at a different rate and caused a patchy texture and color. And most important was his conviction that grog destroyed the purity of the porcelain.

A few days ago, though, Coleman recalled reading that Michael Cardew suggested using broken bisqued pots to make grog. Coleman wondered if such a bisqued porcelain grog would stop the cracking of his large pots—would strengthen the clay without introducing foreign ingredients.

The first step was to reduce his pieces of bisqued porcelain to a proper fineness to make grog. He lacked equipment but Tom Tibbs had relatives who owned a clay-mixing factory with a lab grinder. Despite a mere two-inch opening, the grinder did the job. Tibbs ground the bisque down to particles ranging in size from dust to window screen mesh.. He and Tom also used a hand extruder to pug out hunks of fresh clay that could be dried quickly, bisqued, and run through the grinder. The grog produced was like sand in consistency and white in color. Coleman added 100 pounds of it to his clay at once.

"And it's working! It is really working," he said with a broad smile. "Of course, we have to wait and see . . . but it's looking awfully good. I've cut my losses on the large pots to almost zero the last couple days. Hope we can keep going like this."

Coleman went on enthusiastically: "This could be a very important step, you know, finding a way to stop cracks without destroying the clay. Now I admit that the porcelain is not absolutely pure this way, but I've got to do it—besides, the grog is made from exactly the same clay . . . you can't even see it—it's undetectable."

He resumed working and I looked around the studio, my eyes coming to rest on a table filled with exceptional vases, bowls, jars—some between two and three feet tall. A ginger jar about 30 inches high and with a swelling belly at least 36 inches around commanded attention. The shape was Coleman's current favorite and he had just finished this piece, which had the luminous, grey-white glow I had come to associate with tautly stretched, slightly moist porcelain. I looked inside, and despite the jar's height and girth, its thickness at mid-wall appeared no more than three-eighths of an inch, and perhaps slightly more than one-half inch at the mouth; I could not tell about the base.

The nearby vases, which were about 18 inches high, had thinner walls of course. Their trumpet-shaped mouths tapered to long, slim waists that flared out again to trumpet-shaped bases. The balance between the top and bottom flares was so delicate that some pieces looked in danger of toppling. I touched one and it held its place solidly.

Tom said total shrinkage of each pot, in the bisque and the final kiln, would run to ten to twelve percent.

Coleman went into the rear room where the small downdraft kiln was hot with a test firing, which included two teapots Coleman especially liked. I joined him but heavy draughts of carbon monoxide chased us back to the front room. He returned to the wheel for awhile, then rechecked the kiln. Flames spurted out as he pulled bricks from peep holes and saw the No. 10 cones glowing orange-white and bending. The temperature was 2300° F. "That's nearly where I like to take it—close to twenty-three-fifty, just short of turning the stuff to glass," Coleman said.

When the last cone was down he hurried to the gas tanks some 50 feet outside the studio and shut off the fuel line to the kiln. Then, with a pro-longed yell he galloped back, hurdling a pile of wood and coiled wire, throwing open doors, and shouting for everyone (Elaine, the boys, two dogs, and me) to clear the way. He reached the kiln and switched it off. Then, with a grin he turned and explained breathlessly that he had made it before the gas in the line was used up. If he had been late, he added, there could have been a damaging back-blast inside the kiln.

I inquired whether this race against the gas involved a purism—as with the use of grog—which ruled out doing things the easy way, such as having one person turn off the gas outside and shout to a partner inside who then turned off the oven.

"The fact is, sir," Coleman replied, "it could be done that way—but there is no exercise in that, and it's so common and dull—I needed some excitement."

The kiln would be allowed to cool for only about 12 hours before it was opened.

The phone rang for Coleman and he returned from it saying that he had to prepare a flyer for the Seattle exhibition. The gallery manager wanted 1,500 copies 21 days before the opening so they could be addressed and mailed well ahead of time. The flyer would be the main form of advertising the event. Coleman said he was considering having a flyer in full color for the first time.

Throughout the day, his mood was congenial as he answered my questions and discussed his work and his attitudes.

He said the pressures of potting and sales and his natural intensity had compelled him to try many means of relaxing. None had given a final answer. "Booze and dope are not my thing. I tried them, but they took too much out of me, even though I stopped short of the really heavy stuff. It scared me—I saw too many people freak out. Some are still gone—blank spaces in their heads.

"And yoga and Zen were not it for me either," he said. "I believe in their traditions, the ideas, the disciplines—but I can't go the whole route with them. I was pretty serious with yoga for quite a while, but as a regular practice it demanded more time than I could give it. The meditation was a help—still is; I combine it with running; slip into it sometimes and sail along for miles and am hardly aware of it. Swimming is good for me, too—I did a lot of swimming as a kid.

"Of course, I've been hyper as far back as I can remember. Been going to doctors since I was a kid for tension and depression. Geez, the depression—had it for 20 years. Even when I was a kid I couldn't get organized in the mornings—didn't want to do anything. Glum. Down. Miserable. It'd take an hour to get going. Now I'm weird in the mornings, really. I mope around, hate the idea of going to work, just can't get myself to go in there (the studio)—hate it. But I always get there somehow," he said, his face portraying the depression he has just described.

"But that's the way I am. I can't help it and I'm trying to deal with it. Still, I like to socialize and even though I'm not a good salesman, I can sell my pots," he said, smiling now. "I like that. Some potters also get all wound up in theories and philosophizing; they go on and on about their pots and everything else—so much that they hardly throw pots anymore. The fact is they really don't want to throw pots, they just want all that cool philosophy and laid-back lifestyle. That's okay with me, but they shouldn't hassle me when I make pots and go sell 'em."

Coleman had told me once that he did not necessarily enjoy making pots any longer, that it had become a technical job. But this was impossible to believe after seeing the pieces he made and knowing the concern that he put into them. One broiling afternoon, temperature well over 100 degrees, he had worked on two large pieces for one hour after another. Sweat dripped off his face into the clay as he worked each pot to the shape he wanted, perfecting the mouth, smoothing the exterior walls with the small sponge and ribs. If the whisper of a throwing line remained, it was because he wanted it there.

I referred to this today but he would acknowledge receiving only a mild aesthetic pleasure working the clay. He repeated an earlier claim that he made pots mainly to decorate them.

"That's why I think of the pot as a canvas," he said. "Shaping—bisqueing—trimming clay is the equivalent of stretching a canvas—a means to an end. You'll see. Wait 'til we start decorating; now *that* is something!"

I had never seen him decorate, but I still was not convinced that throwing gave him as little satisfaction as he claimed. I guessed this claim was part of some game with himself, but for the moment he was absolutely serious. It was not a joke, his joking usually followed certain patterns, such as earlier this day. He was trimming pots, and as he finished a foot he signed the leathery clay "Thomas Coleman" in flowing script, using a nail as a stylus.

"'ere we are, matey," he said, holding it up, "me most important tool—this 'ere nile. Gotta sign me bloody nyme. Blimey, only reason I make the bleedin' pots is ta put me nyme on 'em. Ha-haw! Lucky, I'd say, that I can spell it proper."

Our ensuing dialogue produced several minutes of illuminating discussion on "the 10-penny nail and its multiple uses for the potter—from signing pots to cleaning boot treads to picking peanut morsels from the molars."

As for his serious talk that went astray, I wondered if that was a case of one statement leading to another until words and emotions preceded thought. The words just rolled out— amused, hurt, angry, whatever—and got carried along on their own momentum. There was no question that

Coleman liked to talk. It was part of the reason the sales room which had been at the studio was closed. He said three or four customers might come in a day and he would spend so much time with them that he could not get his work done. And at least half the people never bought anything, just hung around and talked. "The truth is, though, I enjoyed it," he said.

The most difficult visitor to the studio, however, came from the Internal Revenue Service. "A kid—younger than me—showed up here for an audit one day and says, 'Awright, now, we found out about you artists— yeah!—all making thirty or forty thousand a year and paying taxes on *ten*! Well, those days are over, I'm here to tell you!'" Coleman waved his hands around a good deal as he went on. "Geez, this guy wants us to keep track of every gallon of gas, every shred of anything. Write it down in one of these little books, he says. I tried but finally told him 'no way; we are doing everything possible, far better than most people, to keep track of our money. This is all we can do—if you want better, *you* do it.' God, it was awful. What an experience. We were clean, too. Everything was fine, but what hell we had to go through to make 'em believe it."

Among the most pleasant recent visitors, he said, were potter Cynthia Bringle, from Penland, North Carolina, and her sister. Cynthia was in Portland to conduct a workshop and they came to the Colemans' for dinner. "I really enjoyed them," Tom said, "fine people. They had this nice way of talking and right away I got back my ol' southern accent. 'I shore 'nuff did enjoy those gals. How ya all doin' now? Why that's fine, jus' real good. Shore glad to have ya. Drop by any ol' time.'"

The conversation, as usual, kept jumping from one thing to another. "What's going to be the title of the book?" Tom asked.

"Nothing's definite yet," I said, "but the working title is *Tom Coleman: Master Potter*."

"It's what?" Coleman said, stopping his work and looking sharply over at me.

I repeated the working title and he screwed up his mouth and twisted his eyebrows into a dark frown. "You're joking," he said, "Master Potter? *Master*?"

"What's wrong with that? Isn't that a standard designation for an experienced potter, or craftsman of any kind?"

"Maybe so, in that sense," he said, "but, I mean, there's only a few potters in the whole world that I think of as masters...that's heavy...I mean, you put master on there and I'll never live it down."

I assured him there was nothing definite and we had plenty of time to think of something. This led to a few minutes of competition to make the most ridiculous title, and then into old jokes and limericks and lines of poetry and whatever else came to mind. I mentioned a favorite quotation (from art lover J.M. Thorburn, as quoted by philosopher Susanne K. Langer) that said, "All the genuine deep delight of life is in showing people the mud-pies you have made...." I could not remember the rest of it exactly.

"Mud-pies?" Coleman said. "Hey, yeah, mud-pies! That's pots all right. I get a kick out of makin' 'em, and a kick out of showin' 'em around. Yessiree, mud-pies is right!"

August 30, Canby—Coleman's handyman friend, "Ol' Ed," was leaning against his pickup and chatting when I arrived in mid-morning; Coleman was moaning over a headache acquired celebrating Elaine's birthday the previous night with potter friends at a Greek restaurant. As soon as Ed left, however, Tom went straight to work on his largest pieces.

"I spent nearly two hours throwing just one of these jars yesterday," he said. "It was the biggest pot I have ever thrown in my life—and it busted. Yeah, I pushed it too far—got it too thin, too much tension, and . . . slump! Whoosh! The air went out of it like its soul had flown. You could hear it. Yep, it just kind of sighed and crumpled up—and there really was something like a gasp. That's true! . . . Makes you wonder, eh, amigo?" His voice trailed off as he arched his eyebrows in the manner of old grade-B movie villains.

Then he sighed, turned back to the wheel and said, "Damn, don't know why I do that. Seems like I'm pushing too hard lately. You know, it always seems like I want to ruin 'em. Sorta knew right along that I was going to bust that big one yesterday, and—sure enough—I kept fooling with it 'til it did. I do that lately." He laughed.

That was the last burst of talk for quite a while. He worked on the clay with longer unbroken concentration than I had ever seen.

These large pots were being thrown in two sections and then fitted together. He used that method when a piece would be too tall for him to reach the interior base, or when it required too much clay to center easily. He had set up a borrowed wheel similar to his own in the center of the main workroom. He began work there, using about one-third of the 40- to 50-pound mound of clay that would go into the whole pot. Coleman quickly threw this portion into a bowl-shape about 15 inches high but with no floor, so it was like a collar. This would be the upper section of the finished jar, the open bottom being inverted to become the mouth.

He took measurements of the piece with a caliper and then moved to his usual wheel, threw the remaining clay into a bowl slightly taller and thicker than the first one, and with a floor. His main concerns up to this point, he explained later, were the basic shapes, the match-up between the two sections (which he checked a few times with the caliper), and the strength of the bottom portion (being certain that it could support the top). He paid close attention also to the comparative dryness of the two sections, because if one was wetter when they were joined the two pieces would shrink differently and ruin the pot's shape. For this reason, when he finished throwing the second section he trained a small electric fan on it to make it equal in dryness, or stiffness, with the piece that was already done. While the fan blew, he leveled the bowl's lip with a needle tool, scored it, and applied a thin coat of slip.

Returning to the collar-like first section, Coleman bent down carefully and lifted it from the wheel. It was nearly as big around as a peach basket, and presumably very hard to handle, but Tom's fingertips were so positioned on the clay that as he straightened his body the collar did a magnificently slow end-over-end twirl. This was so perfectly timed that just as Coleman achieved a standing position the twirl was completed and the bottom of the piece, still stuck to the bat, settled into place as the top.

Then, continuing to hold the slightly moist, wavering thin collar in his fingertips, Coleman glided across the dusty floor with the controlled grace of a dancer carrying a ballerina and stopped before the other wheel. Pausing only briefly to make a visual match of the two pieces, Tom slowly lowered the big circle of clay onto the one upon the wheel. They fit perfectly.

Coleman smiled and murmured to himself, cut away the bat with a wire, and switched the wheel on slow speed while nudging the combined pieces onto center.

I stood in amazement. It was as if a choreographed dance had occupied the minute or less that it took to bring the two halves of the pot together. For once, however, I said nothing, sensing somehow that there were no words Coleman or I could say that could improve and not detract from that unexpected minute of art. (I did mention it several months later, and Coleman did not recall the particular incident but said he understood my reaction: "The first time I saw Creitz do that I was staggered, frightened; I thought I would never be able to do it. For a long time I couldn't sleep the night before I had to do that. Ha. Now I just do it. Makes you think how far you've come.")

Coleman showed no awareness of it and continued at work. He scored all around the pot across the seam where the pieces joined so that it looked as if the sections had been stitched together. Then, after working over the surface with a metal rib, he shifted inside. His entire arm disappeared as he reached in to make a pass up the interior wall. Six more times he went in up to his shoulder, and the pot grew taller. He finished up on the outside, smoothing the connecting seam until it was invisible.

Coleman worked extra hard for forms that were simple and smooth because he wanted that kind of surface to paint on. When he threw a piece for an hour or more, he helped sustain the clay by cleaning slip off the surface once every two passes; the metal rib skimmed off excess water that otherwise would soak into the clay and contribute to its collapse. That rib was used also to eliminate encircling lines left by his fingers; these lines could develop into slight ruts that attracted the fingers and weakened the pot; such lines also interfered with brushwork.

Another technique for extending throwing time was to add water when it was needed by squeezing a sponge just ahead of his fingers. The sponge did not touch the clay and was squeezed just enough to wet but not drench the clay. This replaced the full—and weakening—bath usually given a pot before each new pass. Coleman made a point, too, of keeping excess water off the floor of a piece, sponging it up whenever it puddled.

As for his standard hand techniques in throwing, Tom centered by pressing with the fingers and heels of his hands, keeping the inner palm out of contact with the clay. He opened with the fingers of his left hand on top, right hand at the side. He made passes with the inside (left) hand using just one fingertip, which he said gave him more control than the more common knuckle-type methods. This finger pushed out a ridge or lump of clay and fingertips on the outside (right) hand came to a level about one-eighth to one-fourth of an inch below that ridge. In making the pass, the fingers lifted the ridge between them, maintaining a steady finger placement plus out-and-upward pressure from start to finish of the pass.

Coleman said he learned to rely on the fingertip style of throwing because standard methods were so difficult for him.

During the first break in work, I asked if he knew how he wanted to glaze and decorate each pot now.

"No, I don't. I'm not considering finishes yet. I'll have to see all the pieces together, ready to be decorated. Then I'll look at each one individually—longer as individuals—and try to get the feel of each piece, the texture, shape, and so on. Then I'll try to see what belongs on it. And only at that point will I start making decisions about glazes and colors and painting."

After Tom returned to work, the phone rang and he asked me to answer. A youngish woman's voice said brightly that she represented a new gallery that was being opened and wanted to talk to Tom Coleman. I said he was working and she said she would hold on. Tom reluctantly left the wheel and took the phone.

After about three minutes of conversation, I heard him say, "Sure, I already told you I could find a pot for you to put up.... Yes, but I'm not going down that way soon.... Right, I'm working for a show. Sure, but that'd take a whole day to just go down there and back.... No, no, I said you're *welcome* to a pot. I'll get it ready. And if I find someone going that way I'll send it along.... No, I cannot deliver it myself.... I'm *working!*"

He jammed the phone into its cradle and cursed. "She's opening this gallery and wants me to bring a piece. It's a 200-mile round trip and she says I should bring it—'It'll give you some excellent exposure.' Oh, man, what BS. And this happens all the time. Oh yeah, some gallery people are really rough with artists, potters, whoever. Hell, big deal—exposure, huh, at her place? Haw! I don't even know her.... But a lot of 'em talk to you like that—treat you like a flunky hired hand. Not just me—oh, no—I've heard some of the biggest potters, big painters, talked to like that—'Do this, do that'—like they are being granted some fantastic favor to have their work displayed by this creep. Imagine! The great artists have to go through that. Oh, man! Wowwwwww...."

A friend phoned a little later and after Coleman resumed work a car with a man and woman pulled up outside the studio. Tom went to meet them, guided them toward the house, and chatted dully and impatiently for about 10 minutes, making nods and grunting responses to their enthusiastic patter. He said he had no pots for sale and escorted them toward their car. Before they had even started the engine, he was back inside the studio.

"Didn't seem to be dear friends," I said.

"This is true—they are leeches. They've gotten pots from me before, sold 'em and never paid me. Did it more than once. They're always *into* some new thing. Now it's El Aye—they live in El Aye. You got to say El Aye, right? Not Los Angeles, no-no it is El Aye, man, hoo—ray."

Coleman used relatively little of the current hip jargon. He sometimes inflected faddish words like *into* just enough to show some disdain for them without making a speech.

He returned to work but 15 minutes later another car pulled up and Coleman put both hands to his head and muttered, "What is going on today?" This time a former student was just dropping by. Coleman exchanged pleasantries, offered him a seat and resumed work. The fellow was nearly Tom's age and hung around the rest of the day, wandering in and out of the studio and house. Coleman barely spoke to him again, seemed to forget his presence.

In the early afternoon Elaine brought out the day's mail. It included a tabloid-sized newspaper from the Pottery Northwest, Inc. studio in Seattle; the front page banner in inch-high letters said: "COLEMAN TO GIVE WORKSHOP." The story said Tom would conduct a class for advanced students and professionals the day after his show opened in Seattle October 7.

We took time out for a sandwich in the house—a concession to me, I learned later; Tom's preferred lunch was handfuls of peanuts and raisins from large containers kept in the studio.

Back at work, he made more section pots—vases this time, with fluted mouths and fluted bases joined by long slim waists. The finished pieces stood about 30 inches high. After completing one in less than 45 minutes he became more deeply involved with the next one and spent twice that much time. He rarely spoke and the long silence itself became an entity, calling attention to the intense activity within it.

Standing with feet planted wide, Coleman's torso corkscrewed and his left shoulder tilted up so the left arm slipped inside the spinning cylinder up to his armpit. At times his stare was trancelike, eyes bulging from their sockets. With each pass, his inside hand came up—allowing just one fingertip to make contact—and the outside hand, holding the sponge, came with it, lifting clay from the thicker bottom section to the top. Small lumps rose above his fingertips like tiny elevators or small creatures running under a rug.

He leaned back, sighed and muttered that he was getting too much clay in the upper section. But he inserted his arm again, narrowing his hand into a trowel shape so it could squeeze through the narrow waist. He began another pass, his breath a controlled hiss as he nursed a small bulge to the top, where it flowed like liquid into the fluted lip, making a little wobble as it vanished.

His breath burst out and he swore. The pot was not submitting to his control. The top had become larger and grander than he intended—yet he had continued to make passes, pulling more clay to the top, where the mouth now fluted open too widely. Coleman grumbled. And stared. And in the next instant he made a quick movement of his fingers—a magician's gesture, the kind used to pick fire from the air or to produce the missing coin—and from the rim pulled a thin sheath of clay. It had suddenly changed direction, flowing at a 90-degree angle *back* across the pot's mouth. He stopped short of the center, leaving an opening slightly larger than a silver dollar, to which he applied a needle tool. The needle trimmed from the inside edge two doughouts of thin clay that melted like Dali-clocks when he plucked them up and away.

Using rib and sponge, Coleman smoothed the walls and half-closed mouth, then leaned back in his chair, frowned and shook his head.

"Naw, not right," he said gruffly. "Damned thing kept fighting me. Gee-*zus* that is *work*! Too much clay in the top, got top heavy . . . out of propor-tion . . . yeah . . . isn't it?"

I thought it was terrific. The shape did not appear top heavy to me—the reversal of the lip's excess flare had fixed it. Now the clay seemed ready to rise, soar up on its own, and was held in check by the flare of the base. The tension was palpable. I was standing back from the piece, and Coleman was close, which could account for his feeling it was wrong—or maybe I was misjudging it. Anyway, I told him I thought the vase was excellent.

Coleman stood, backed up a few feet and stared at the vase. He looked tired and a bit sullen, but there was also a determined, angry flash in his eyes. "You really like this bitch, huh?" he said. "Well, I don't know . . . maybe it's not so bad, looks a little better from back here—I keep saying I should get a big mirror so I can see these large pieces while I'm working on 'em. But I don't know about this one. It's mean, *really* mean . . . glad you like it, but it took something out of me. I don't know if I want to do any more today or not."

He took a little stroll around the studio, then lifted the piece from the wheel. "'Tiz a vawz, sir," he said. "I do believe 'tiz properly called a vawz." He carried it to a table—faking a stumble and the start of a fall en route—and stood its sweeping curves beside the swollen roundness of a ginger jar and other large pots. In the shadowy light the table looked like a cemetery full of tombstones or a squad of oddly-matched ghosts—rows of smooth forms, each different yet with the same glossy grey-white glow. Behind them, a cranky-looking rusty woodstove stood like an octopus with reddish-black arms and legs shooting in all directions from double-barreled fire chambers. Tom had said that in winter the heat roared out. At the moment, however, it was a cool and spidery overseer of ghostly troops of porcelain.

Coleman seemed to become more tolerant of the last vase as minutes passed. He did stop work for the day, however, and announced it was time to retire on the porch by the pond and have a relaxed drink. As he arranged his tools, I remarked how quiet it had been in the studio.

"Yeah, it was," he said. "I'm usually more quiet when I'm decorating, have to concentrate all the time then. When I'm throwing I usually talk like crazy, drive people right up the wall. And I'm messy, too. Yep, very messy—it's better to be neat and clean, but I'm a filthy mess and what the hell has that got to do with anything anyway." He twitched his shoulders, glanced around the room, took a deep breath and let out a yell:

"Yeeeeeeahooooooo! Hey! I mean dammit! Fan-tas-tic, right? Right now, at this moment, it is fantastic! I love it—love the feel of that clay. Drive you nuts—really! Hey, it is a terrible cliche to say that it's like some beautiful woman, but it really is something sensual . . . and mysterious. That sounds so phony, but it's true. And some people say the greatest time for porcelain is now, right now when it has that pearly-grey sheen and kind of glows from inside. That surface feels almost like skin . . . kind of clings to your hand. . . ." He shook his head, grinned, and said, "I'll tell you this: it sure beats any work I've ever done. . . . Course I haven't done much. Haw!"

September 1 and 5, Portland—Coleman came twice to Portland to pick out photographs from some I had taken that might work on a flyer for the Seattle show. He had dropped his plan to have it done in full color when the printer estimated 1,500 copies would cost at least $480. Black and white with one color would cost $85.

Coleman said Tom Tibbs was going to have his flyer done in color despite the high cost. Coleman had invited Tibbs and his wife, Julie, to join the Seattle show, reasoning that he and Elaine would not need the gallery's two rooms and that the Tibbses could use the smaller rear room. They were expected to have about 30 or 40 pots.

Seeing Coleman outside the studio, wearing a sweater and fresh jeans, reminded me of my first impression of him as merely a good-looking young fellow. I remarked now that his most obvious problem was that he did not look like an artist as popularly conceived. He was without beard or mustache; did not wear bizarre clothes—not even his clayey boots and grimy workpants; behaved tolerably well in public, except for occasional unexplained outbursts of laughter.

"That's right," he said. "What do you think I tried so hard to grow a beard for—and all I got was scraggly fuzz. Lookin' like a kid, how you going to get respect? Every show there's a little old lady who says, 'Why, are you the Tom Coleman who made all these nice pots? Well, isn't that a surprise. So young. I can hardly believe you are the one. Arthur, come over here, this is the boy who made that nice vase . . . the one on the piano, Arthur, beside the picture of Beatrice and Harold.' Ha, it always happens. I just tell 'em I'm still in high school."

He left for the printer's saying the flyer had to be done in 10 days.

September 6, Canby—For the first time in my visits, Elaine worked in the studio. She was making hand-built boxes at a table next to a window in the main room. A higher table nearby was covered by a sheet of clay rolled out like bakery dough. Darker and heavier than the clay Tom was using, this was the coursest of the three porcelain formulas the Colemans currently had in regular use. I had asked Tom if he guarded his formulas and he said he gave them away. Was it the same way chefs gave away recipes—leaving out one or two key ingredients?

"Naw, I give 'em out pretty much as I use them," he said. "Of course, I'm always changing, adjusting; that's the thing about my formula, you have to keep alert, adapt it to where you are, what you are doing, the availability of ingredients—or the fluctuations in them. That's why you've got to *know* the fundamentals: your materials and your work. It's the only way you can get the best out of any formula. I've spent so damned much time with the porcelain by now that I know it as well as anybody around here—probably better. And decorating? Well, that's art. So what can anybody do about all that? If they want my formulas, want to copy me—okay, come ahead, good."

We had talked also about what constituted porcelain. Tom said, "I don't think porcelain can be narrowed down to one definition for everyone, but a few things must always be there for me. One is translucency, the clay's ability to transmit light. Second, the body has got to be dense, vitreous almost to a glasseous state. And third is that the clay body be white or grey-white and not develop iron spots."

Were some porcelains much easier to handle than others?

"Well, possibly, but any time you deal with a clay that will meet those requirements, you're going to have difficulties. First off, it'll be soft and sticky, very difficult to shape and control. It almost drives you crazy when you are beginning. Maddening. And the only way to overcome that is to handle the stuff constantly; work with it and work with it. You just have to find out how to make it respond—you must figure out your own ways of dealing with it."

Elaine's hand-building clay was made from a commercial formula that could be used thick as well as thin and dried evenly without cracking. It was also adequate for throwing plates, mugs and smaller pots, but tended to fall back into itself on taller pieces. Tom had two more porcelain formulas—one for pots using up to 25 pounds of clay, the second for the larger section pots.

Elaine's table was beside the octopus-like stove. Tom was at his usual place near the front door. When I arrived he was cordial yet somewhat distant. Several persons—Tom among them—had warned me I might find it difficult to be present as he moved deeper into the work because he got tense and nervous, had moody flights of temperament and depression. My response was that if he did not mind my presence, I would like to see him work as much as possible.

On this day he seemed touchy and inward-looking; I sensed something amiss, out of synchronization—as if a transparent wall stood between us and did not impair vision but delayed our words a beat or two.

Then, while I was in my usual orbit, photographing around Tom's wheel, he fetched a handful of peanuts from a tin near Elaine and in passing made a critical remark about the way she was finishing the corner of a box. Then he stepped over to her table, examined the offending piece and insisted that it was too thick and must be fixed. She said a few words I could not hear, then Tom found fault with the fit of the lid on another box. He shook his head and said, "We simply can't have this kind of work."

I sensed embarrassment on Elaine's part but it may have been my own. I wondered if my presence complicated their usual work routine. Tom commented briefly further; Elaine said nothing.

A bit later he joined me where I was looking at some drying pottery. There was a total of about 75 pieces bisque-fired and a dozen from a glaze test firing. These included the piece he had wanted to put on a full-color flyer—an apple green celadon teapot—and another favorite, a cane-handled red teapot. He said the red was the result of very long and arduous struggle. This pot's lid, however, had shrunk too much and did not fit; he would make several new lids, expecting one to be perfect. Also among the finished pieces were a covered jar decorated with cherries and a hexagonal bowl with grapes. These were the first such finished pieces I had seen. I said I liked them and Coleman said he did too, although they were no longer favorites—"I've been doing these awhile; they're almost standards now. I'm kind of tired of 'em."

I tried teasing him about the "Thomas L. Coleman" sign at the driveway. I had not mentioned it before and now it just popped into my head. I remarked that it had a nice pompous touch, elegantly egotistical.

"Oh, yeah, the sign," he said. "So interesting that you noticed it . . . . Clever. You're the first person to notice it . . . ."

"How's that . . . ?"

"Hell! *Everybody* notices that—everybody asks about it. Elaine's father made it for my birthday; he wanted it put up, so we did. He was supposed to make another one with 'Elaine' on it to go up, too, but he had a stroke. He's been in bed most of the time ever since, never got the second sign done. So, there I am . . . alone and proud, sir, proud."

So I had bumbled into family affairs and embarrassed myself, now feeling awkward over having used the sign—smugly considered as a bit of vanity—to bring Coleman down a bit.

We did not linger on it, but it made me wonder whether I was a contributor to the discordant mood. It was quiet as I made photographs of Tom throwing round shapes the size of grapefruit. Then Elaine left the studio about noon and Tom said, "Doggone it, she's upset—my fault. I know it . . . made her angry. I get so damned critical sometimes. I should keep my mouth shut."

I remarked that my presence probably had not helped matters, and she may not have liked being criticized in front of a virtual stranger; most people would not.

"Yeah . . . yeah, I was pretty bad. I just got going and it got out of hand."

When she returned the mood seemed more relaxed. But then I was taking pictures in the storeroom when I overheard Tom exclaim, "Elaine! What is this? This lid is simply not right. What the hell is wrong today?"

"Don't start coming down on me, Tom!" she snapped back this time. "Dammit! Don't get so heavy with me . . . ."

Later I was to hear such exchanges end in laughter or ribald name-calling, but this day they did not. Following some lower-pitched muttered words, the Colemans moved apart, said no more. When I returned to the front room Tom remarked that things were becoming "a little tense" as they approached decorating and firing. "We've got a fair number of pots at this point but we need more. We've got to stop making pots on the 15th (of September) in order to stay on schedule. And we can lose a lot in firing—cracks, explosions—your never know exactly what will come out, particularly with these larger pots. I've never made so many this big. And don't forget that we've got the new kiln—never fired porcelain in it before. Never! We did some stoneware this summer, but that's all. So, the ol' pressure is abuilding. We stop throwing the 15th and go hard after the decorating. . .then the firing."

How many pieces did they expect to lose.

"Right now you just can't tell how many pots will make it. But you know some are going to be lost—busted, misfired or something."

I pressed for an educated guess on the losses.

"Well, we've been at this a pretty long time now, so it shouldn't be too bad. We ought to get out, say 75 per cent or better. But, remember, I've never put porcelain in this kiln. So there are some important unknowns. We'll just have to wait and see."

Shortly before I left for the day, Tom was tight-lipped at the wheel, working a bowl thinner and thinner. He stretched the piece ever more tautly. . .until it seemed to come unstrung, wobbled, and fluttered crazily. Coleman snapped off the electric power, slammed into the ruined pot with both hands, whacking it again and again. Then he sat still, looked up, and said, "That felt good!"

September 15, Canby—This was supposed to be the last day of throwing pots, but Tom had to go to Portland. Elaine was working alone in the studio, where chalky white and pinkish bowls, vases, jars, urns, bottles and boxes covered tables and racks in each room. Elaine said everything seemed to be going well, and that while the boys were in school she could spend a few hours building pieces. She longed to spend more time at it.

Most of her pieces took a half day or more to construct and longer to incise. She used a variety of implements for the decoration, including a set of dental tools. Elaine spent hours—sometimes a whole day or two—carving on one of Tom's covered bowls. All of her designs were improvised and sought to be strong yet subordinate to the form of the pot. Among her most striking works were close-ups of flowers and birds which had an elegantly abstract quality that enhanced the pottery more than I had thought possible.

I asked how she would describe Tom as a potter.

"He's a good potter—very good," she said. "He's more conscientious, more of a perfectionist than other potters. He never leaves a piece until he has gone to the final edge, final smoothness. He must finish every detail—always. He's just good. Naturally, I think he's the best," she concluded with a smile.

She spoke with reserve, perhaps to establish that her regard for Tom's work was not simply because he was her husband. But when I mentioned that some potters had told me Tom's work was too smooth, too perfect in form, lacked a "funky" quality they admired, Elaine's reserve faded.

"Well, no, of course Tom's work isn't funky if you mean a little bit sloppy or careless, or kind of unfinished," she said quickly. "But if you mean deliberately earthy—you know, loose or rough intentionally—then he can be funky anytime. He has been. But that isn't where he's at right now. His porcelain is really refined."

I asked how it was to work with him, considering that he was supposed to be "difficult."

Elaine said he had his ups and downs, but was doing rather well lately, particularly for a show. "I tease him," she said, "that he's just on his good behavior because you are here . . . taking pictures and all that. But he did blow up pretty good the other day, though—ha!—ask him about the lids for the red teapot. You should have been here . . . real fun. He screamed and jumped around for awhile . . . but it wasn't too bad. He's actually okay—best potter I know. Really. Truly."

September 16, Canby—Coleman worked at the throwing wheel most of the day, having been unable to finish on the 15th as planned. He had been invited to attend a visit by Joan Mondale, the U.S. Vice President's wife, to the Contemporary Crafts Gallery and then spent the rest of the day at the printer's and around town collecting information on an event called "ArtQuake," which was being drummed up as Portland's version of the art fairs in places like Bellevue and Los Angeles, and would be held this coming weekend. Tom disliked interrupting work for the show, but he and Elaine felt they should participate. "These things can be good for the art community if they are handled right—the one at Bellevue is a real winner," Tom said. "Of course it'll take some time to get going here, but this is a start, we ought to support it—also, we might make some money." They would share a booth with the Tibbses and sell the OPW pots they had made together. The fair would run from Friday to Sunday evening in the business heart of the city; all vehicular traffic would be halted and the streets given over to art and craft and food, and bands, a circus, and dancing.

Meanwhile, Tom proclaimed that the day at hand was absolutely the last to make pots for Seattle. He began by trimming leather-hard pieces to be bisqued. Clay spurted up in long grey curls and in tiny chips as he used various trimming tools to sharpen edges, clean up feet, improve rims, remove dents, knicks and scratches.

He used his fingers to "close the clay"—a technique inspired by Korean methods of trimming, in which pots were turned opposite the direction in which they were thrown. This closed clay particles which had been opened up in throwing. Coleman did not have a reversible wheel so he rubbed his fingertips "against the grain" on the foot of each pot. He said this realigned particles and helped prevent surface cracks in drying and firing.

As he worked, he gave a short lecture about the importance of trimming: "It has got to be done, the bottom of a pot is important. You should give it the same kind of concern, care, attention, whatever you want to call it, that you give the top of the pot. Without that, your pot simply isn't finished. Still," he said, flicking a long curl of clay from his cutting blade, "trimming is trimming—routine, no fun. But tomorrow—aha!—the decorating begins! And then—and *then*—the big kiln. Yessir, that big ol' Minnesota Flattop—that's going to be *some* experience."

I asked what would be the main difference between this new kiln and his old ones.

"Before, we had to run everything through the small kiln—took up to 20 firings for one show. But now we might make it in only three or four, *if* we're lucky. That'll be something...big loads! Of course, if a firing goes wrong, we lose a lot of pots...."

Elaine was out of the studio this morning and I inquired about her work.

"She is really coming along fast," Tom said. "I've got to admit I'm surprised. Maybe I'm tough on her, and I know I've held her back, but right now she is doing some fantastic stuff. Her celadons in the last test firing were better than mine. Oh yes—the color was excellent, the pieces were very, very successful. And the boxes are solid, getting better all the time. She could be a terrific potter when she gets the chance to spend more time at it."

Later, he mentioned that the workshop he would conduct in Seattle would pay him $150. A nationally known potter could make up to $1,000 plus expenses on some workshops, he said.

Would he like to do that?

"You mean go around and give workshops...for a thousand bucks? Don't know, why not? It wouldn't be bad to get some of that bread for awhile...and travel too. Go around and see the country, see what other people are doing, making. God, I'd love to do that—I've hardly been anywhere. Nowhere. I'd love to see what's going on. I'd just go around some and not worry all the time about money. Go here, go there—see this guy's work, that guy's. Just talk to people. I'd love that."

We moved to the back room and he kept talking while checking the material he used to prevent pots from sticking on his silicon carbide kiln shelves. This problem of sticking—spalling—was not solved by the washes usually applied to shelves. The washes flaked off, which was destructive because after each firing he turned his shelves end-to-end and over, to prevent sagging—and the flakes would fall into pots. So he put a dusty, resin-like substance on the shelves, and the tiny grains served as minuscule ball bearings between the pots and shelf. The grains did not melt and were easily brushed away or vacuumed when not wanted.

He worked late, but in good humor, anticipating the decorating. The next two days would be dull, though, because it would be mostly glazing, he said, "that's nothing to see—but don't miss it after that."

September 18, Portland—Coleman said by phone that he had some minor problems—the oxides and glazes were not quite right—but he expected everything to be corrected in a day or so. Then the decorating would go ahead full speed.

He mentioned having a long visit with Bill Creitz, his former teacher whom he described as the number one potter around the area in the late '60s. "He had everybody going crazy trying to catch him; was making fifty thousand bucks or more every year in those days. Then he moved to California, went berserk making money, and spending it. But then—I don't know exactly—something happened to his marriage; he came back here last year to make what he calls 'pots in the true way'—wood fire, heavy Korean-style shapes and textures, the rougher and heavier, the better. He's not selling much and claims he doesn't care, but I don't know . . . so there you are, this making pots is a great life."

September 19, Canby—A pot stood atop an overturned bucket on the wheelhead when I arrived, and Tom sat facing the pot, a table within arm's reach. It was filled with bottles, jars and glasses of oxides, and brushes, rags, bats, sprayers, tubes, cans and several items I could not identify. Another larger table held several glazed pots waiting to be decorated and a few that had already been painted—the grey-brown oxides making them look as if they had been daubed with mud. It was impossible for me to visualize them finished because I did not know how the various oxides would respond to the firing. At the moment they reminded me of looking at negative-color film, which the untrained eye sees as a confusing blur of orange-brown with touches of blue-green. Most of the oxides looked muddy brown with some dull green and white.

Coleman said the oxides he was using today included a black stain, rutile, iron oxide, copper carbonate, two cobalts, and a light blue wash. He said they would produce fired colors of gold, green, purple-mauve, grey-blue, dark blue, black and various combinations of these.

Tom fidgeted in his chair and eventually sat very still, staring at the pot, wrinkling his brow, nibbling his lips. He mumbled to himself—"Hummm, maybe a...let's see...willow tree?... Yeah...try one...no...oh, sure, go ahead, why not...?"—then picked through two brush-filled bottles to find the right sumi-style tip.

Turning to the pot—a wide-mouthed roundish piece the size of a basketball—he gripped his right wrist and forearm with his left hand, pressed his left elbow on his knee. Holding the brush in a variation of a classic sumi grip, he poised his right hand above the pot and revolved it as on a swivel: fingers and brush made short sharp jabs in the air, suggesting a tiny shadow boxer, as he rehearsed his opening strokes.

He dipped his brush in oxide and began to paint. Each stroke was deliberate yet swift—a single sustained motion, its mark not to be retouched or worked over. The brush flicked out in a rapid series of arcs, dips, twists and each left a distinctive streak of dark oxide. After two or three dozen strokes, Coleman took a rest, inspected the work closely, then resumed painting. The next time he rested the marks had swirled up and nearly around the pot, creating an unmistakable willow tree, its billowing droopiness aslant in a breeze.

Finished with it and pleased, Coleman laughed exuberantly and did a little jig as he whisked the pot to the rear table and put another bowl atop the bucket-easel.

Coleman turned the bowl around several times, said "cherries?" and began to paint. The bowl would fit comfortably in a person's cupped hands and within three or four minutes he had applied four different oxides in a flurry of non-stop painting. The strokes were shorter and more tightly controlled than for the willow tree. This time his fingers did most of the work. The tips of the brushes set color upon color—small circles and arcs made cherries and leaves, and tiny squares put on top of them made patches of reflection. To finish it he turned on the wheel, held a brush in one spot as the pot spun—and laid a stripe of color all around the rim.

Next came a two-foot-high vase which he attacked with feathery sumi-strokes—a twist here and a zig-zag there made several knuckles which long parallel lines connected to depict nodes of bamboo. It was done in about one-half hour.

He then faced another basketball-sized bowl, pursed his lips, sniffed, wriggled about, stretched, scratched, sighed, and finally stood up. "I gotta go outside," he said, "be right back."

He returned shortly carrying freshly uprooted weeds, vines, flowers on long stems, leaves and tall grasses. He sorted through them chattering nonsensically, inspected every item and selected one to hold against the window light—against the pot. Coleman squinted and twitched some more, murmured, "Why not . . . we'll do 'er," and started searching for the right brushes.

I inquired about the plant and he yelled across the room: "Hey! Elaine! What's this—what is it? What's it called?"

She came over to examine the long green stem, its thin spikey leaves and delicate purple-white blossom with yellow center. "I think it's a catalonia . . . or catcha-something," she said.

"Why, of course—the ol' katachurian, just as I thought. Exactly what I was telling my curious friend here. This chatanooga plant is my favorite of the multitude of early-blooming autumn perennial weeds which do seem to grow by my back door. All right! Alllll RIGHT! Let's get to work!"

Coleman's blue eyes brightened and his laughter pealed, then shifted into a sinister cackle until he said, "All right my leetle katahunka plant . . . weed . . . flower . . . whatever you are—I yam going to painchew!"

Then he went silent, took a deep breath and picked up the blossom, twirled it between his left thumb and forefinger. He dipped a brush into dark chocolate oxide and painted for half-hour stretches, holding the blossom steadily aloft and saying nothing—aloud; he did mutter to himself. When he broke the position to check his progress, he would lean back-back-back in his castered, spring-backed chair until he was almost laid out flat. One time he sat up, slid off the chair and kneeled. Then with his nose nearly against the pot and eyes squinting, he applied brushstrokes to the underbelly where the stem began. The stemline climbed halfway up the pot and expanded into a cluster of spikey leaves that looked like a small school of Oriental fish, then the stem continued upward to a three-color blossom. Near the end of his work, the silhouette of the real flower and the one on the pot looked almost identical.

He finished this piece about 3 p.m., took a couple of handfuls of peanuts as a delayed lunch, and selected another bowl to decorate. Coleman nearly encircled this one with a double series of sharp lines that first suggested a pine cone and ended up a fern.

The day's last piece was a large platter, which Coleman studied for several minutes before making any marks. Then he sprayed on simple dots and brushed comet tails, looping lips and crescents.

He had to do much more decorating the next day, Tom said, including two pieces for a show in Utah. He also had to make preparations for the ArtQuake fair and give some thought to an article he was to write for *Studio Potter*, one of the country's best known potters' journals, whose editor and a photographer had visited the studio while preparing an article on Oregon potmaking. The editor, Gerry Williams, later asked Tom to write an article telling about himself and his work to run six or eight pages of the magazine. "The deadline is the first week in November, but I don't know, can't even think about it now...too much on my mind. Have to do it after the show opens," Coleman said.

I accompanied him as he puttered around the studio to unwind. He sprayed ash-water on some pieces and touched up others where ash-based decorations had flaked off. Looking around, he said, "Whew, what a mess this place is. I always have a mess—can't seem to help it. I try to keep the place clean, I really do—but it's just filthy and I just work in it like a pig and...I don't know." He walked from room to room, checking on this and that, and muttered to me, "Really dirty, huh? Horrible! We gotta clean it up some." He repeated such remarks several times over the next hour and seemed to get more serious each time. Finally he gave a complete little sermon to Elaine and me about the need for cleanliness in the studio.

Meanwhile, he showed pieces from the most recent test firing. His favorite was a tureen-like covered porcelain with milk-white glaze. Around the belly was a wide, earthy purple-brown-pink belt suggesting gnarled roots and floating islands from which rose leafless trees. The skeletal limbs were black. Just above them glowed a burnished gold ball...circle...sun. It was stunning.

Alongside were two covered jars with ash decorations. Their rich brown colors ranged from dark chocolate to beige, with streaks of mauve and green. The long lines of dripping ash reminded me of an aspen forest. These pieces wanted to be touched and had a pebbly quality—like large-grained leather that was smooth but not slick.

Among other pieces from the firing were boxes of Elaine's. Tom said, "Geezus these are super! I can't get over how good she is getting." The prize was a celadon with double walls—a three-quarter-inch space between the walls—and 10 inches by 10 inches overall; the elegant green glaze was lively without being too bold.

Coleman continued to move around the studio and I followed, taking photos and asking questions. The hardest part of painting was wielding the brushes, he said. "It took me years to learn to do brushwork properly. Applying oxide on a round or curved surface—while you keep perspective—is hard, too. And the only way to learn to use oxides is by experience. Keep at it."

He confessed that some of his glaze and oxide formulas—and application techniques—were kept secret. I recalled his claim that he had no such secrets. He laughed, and said, "Yeah, well, that's right, I don't—except on some very special things."

"Such as?"

"Okay, I'm particularly careful about certain things done to paint beneath a glaze."

"And what if a potter, friend or otherwise, asked for details?"

Coleman grimaced. "Nobody would ask—too pushy," he said.

Then I mentioned his much longer periods of concentration while decorating. He said that decorating caused a different kind of tension in him—he could not talk much because he had to think more; throwing could sometimes be done as if his hands were disembodied and he hardly needed to even watch.

Suddenly he halted our conversation, turned abruptly and hurried into the back room to search among the just-fired pieces. "All right now . . . now we'll see, we'll find out—dammit all, where's that pot?"

He strode back into the main room, hands against his stomach cradling lids. He put the cane-handled red teapot on a table and tried the lids. The first was too small. The next was nearly right but had a slight wobble. The third was cracked. The fourth did not match color. The fifth was perfect.

Tom whirled around, yelling to Elaine, who had already come to watch. "You see, Elaine—you see! I told you one of these would have to work. Look—perfect! Couldn't be better. Fan-tastic! Um, almost, too tight, though, uh, but I can fix that okay . . . ah . . . here . . . see . . . . Oh . . . . Hell! Damn you pot!

As he had demonstrated how smoothly the lid's flange aligned with the pot's flange, a small nub that helped secure the lid cracked off.

Coleman stopped shouting and tried the last two new lids. Neither was adequate and he uttered a string of obscenities. Elaine recommended that he forget that pot—he had made more than a dozen lids and none worked—the red teapot was simply not meant to be.

"Oh-no," Tom said, "oh-no! I am going to make more lids this time—I'll make a dozen more. They'll probably *all* fit. You just wait and see!"

Elaine snorted and said to me, "All I know is this: we should have visitors all the time. You should have seen him the first time on these lids—whew, ran around here like a madman. Did pretty good today, though, didn't you, Tom? How come you don't show John what you are really like. Afraid he'll take pictures? Tell everyone? Ha!"

"Never mind all that," Coleman said with a determined smile, "the red teapot shall be saved. You wait. I'll make a hundred lids if I have to. It's a fine pot, I like that pot. It should have a lid."

August 20, Canby—Coleman decorated all day, chatting amiably during breaks and mentioning more than once that he planned to load and fire the kiln tomorrow. He said he would select about 30 pots in a variety of sizes, shapes, glazes and decorations to test the kiln—"Remember: first time with porcelain."

I described and evaluated the work of various potters I had seen recently and asked for his opinions. On the first one he said, "That sounds about right; pretty close to what he does; 'course, I'll tell you—he used to be one of the great ones, but something happened. Too much success, arrogance—I don't know—maybe he just got tired of it." On another potter—"Hey, that guy used to be a student of mine—terrific, really brilliant, as a potter and intellectually, too. He learned to make such good pots so fast that I was jealous. Really. But he went funny, strange. I haven't seen him for a long time but he must have tried to go too fast or something. Great talent." I mentioned a potter who wrote and put up emotional  blurbs about his pieces and we agreed the results were embarrassing, Coleman adding that the potter was "very capable—really promising. But people go through periods, you know—up, down, do something nutty for awhile. I think now of some potters I really used to look up to—you hardly ever see their stuff anymore. Creitz used to tell me that if a potter could stick it out for the first 10 years he'd be okay. Well, I have, and I'm glad, but it sure isn't getting easier—gets harder all the time to do better... even to make a living."

I brought up a fellow whose latest show had no appeal for me. "Oh well! Of course, sure," Coleman said, "but that was partly just bullheadedness. He is really very big, very good, but he's been on a weird kind of trip—maybe he's smoking too much dope or something. I'm sure he'll pull out, but I agree that this last stuff was gawdawful, everybody said so. I'd be embarrassed to show it; can't understand why he did...."

The phone rang. Tom Tibbs reported that the printer said technical problems would delay the flyer for a few days. Coleman grumbled awhile, then said, "Oh well, my big problem right now is this decorating —the designs are so tough; have to be new all the time and need variety. It's miserable doing the same ones over again. Got to change."

When I left he was staring at another round pot. He looked up and said, "You better be here again in a day or so—we're firing the kiln."

September 22, Portland—The Colemans had loaded the kiln, fired it, and expected to turn it off this evening. They invited my wife, Joyce, and me for dinner. In the morning I phoned Susanna Kuo, the artist-critic whose review had upset Coleman. She was cordial, told me when the review appeared in the *Willamette Week* newspaper and agreed to discuss it after I had read it. A friend at the *Week* provided me a copy. A front page index carried a small photo of a Coleman pot and referred to Kuo's review inside. It took up half a page and began by saying that the three shows under review had opened simultaneously at the Contemporary Crafts galleries and raised questions about what was a good exhibit. It then said:

"A one-man show is quite literally (and legally) the 'publication' of an artist's work, just as publication of a collection of poems sets a poet's work before the public. No less than in a work of literature or music, we should expect the individual pieces in a one-man show to add up to a cohesive and meaningful whole. But perhaps because an art exhibit, in contrast with published literature and music, is not subject to reproduction and therefore is not with us longer than a period of weeks, artists and galleries alike tend to be more casual about these criteria than writers, composers and publishers. Ideally, there should be a sense of purpose behind an artist's choice of materials, techniques and the type of design problems being explored, all adding up to some sort of aesthetic statement."

By these standards, the review said textile artist Reta Miller "takes first place among the three craftsmen," and discussed Miller's exhibit. Next, potter Ron Taylor's raku pots were considered somewhat "charming" and "appealing" but generally lacking in maturity and forcefulness; "Taylor does not seem quite ready for show."

Then beneath the photo of his pot, Tom Coleman was described as—

"a talented potter who has mastered the very difficult art of throwing porcelain, not just small manageable forms, but tall, challenging containers large enough to stand on the floor. With their handsome proportions and their fluid, Japanese-inspired brush work, Coleman's pieces are easy to admire."

I wondered if I had the wrong review; nothing to annoy Coleman here. The text, however, went on:

"And so it may seem perverse of me to criticize Coleman for the very things that many people may regard as his strengths—his prolific output, the multiplicity of his forms and styles, his easy-to-look-at motifs.

"I found his show disappointing because it seems to lack coherence and aesthetic sense of direction. There is a bewildering variety of forms and design: lidded jars, plates, bottles, tea sets, boxes, even a ginger-jar lamp with a porcelain shade. A number of pieces, like a sublime blue-violet jar and a striking large black plate with bold loops and splashes in brown, are one-of-a-kind.

"For the sake of coherence, some of the pieces (no matter how attractive) might better have been omitted. This principle of restraint could also be applied to the decoration of individual pieces. Coleman is probably as skilled with the brush as with the potter's wheel. But if one brushstroke is good, then two or four are better. The prevailing impression is one of *virtuosity* but not *discipline*.

"That Coleman's motifs—bamboo, leaves, grasses, flowers, branches and landscapes—are easy to like is not in itself a criticism. But they do not demand involvement, output from the viewer. And Coleman's apparent restlessness in moving from one decorative approach to another suggests that he himself is not deeply involved with the images he employs. They do not appear to be a natural outgrowth of his own experience.

"If I am hard on Coleman, it is precisely because he is not a second-rate craftsman. The shortcomings I see in his work (restlessness, failure to weed out the irrelevant, lack of restraint, the seductions of attractive, ready-made images) are weaknesses I see in myself, temptations that face all of us who are craftsmen or artists.

"And so, you may say, who really cares whether a show has aesthetic integrity? Besides, it must be a difficult choice, when your livelihood depends on selling your work, whether to make a piece that you know (either consciously or subconsciously) will have obvious appeal as opposed to a more demanding or austere work which is less likely to sell."

Kuo concluded the review with a quotation from art historian Ernst Gombrich:

"There is such a thing as an aesthetic attitude. . . . That is to say, the interest of the public in refinement and in various points . . . an informed public who are appreciative of nuances, who can discriminate in the finest way. . . . Then only do you get an artist who finds it worthwhile to develop his talents and to improve his styles."

My first reading of the article brought a mixed reaction, although, of course, I had not even seen the show so could not possibly judge the review against it. However, I did not agree with some aspects of her premise of shows; and it was shows—not the particular works of the craftsmen—that the review set itself up to consider.

Considering that, I did not understand why Coleman had remained so upset about the review. I could understand his being bothered for awhile, but why months later, unless she had touched extremely sensitive points? Also, I was intrigued that Kuo found his work to be unrestrained and restless while the most serious other criticism I had heard was that it was too restrained. And while Kuo said three times his work was "easy" to look at, the others had said it was stiff and overworked. Later, while driving to Canby, I mulled over Susanna Kuo's reference to selling and wondered how clearly—consciously or subconsciously—most artists distinguished between aesthetic integrity and saleability, and whether that choice was as everpresent and operational as she suggested. Of course, on many occasions it was easily clear, but others were hazy, complex. One reason artists had agents and managers was that sales decisions were better left to businessmen.

Most significantly to me, however, was that Kuo zeroed in on Coleman's dilemma. It seemed to me that her position was sound—for a pure and idealistic goal. For craftsman-artists like Coleman, however, who supported a family of four solely on what they produced, the lines between artistic idealism and practicality were tangled. A choice may require saying no to something equally or even more worthy—as much as saying yes to art.

When Joyce and I reached the studio that evening, Coleman was watching the big kiln closely, checking cones every 15 minutes as the temperature approached 2250° F. The kiln had about 75 cubic feet of interior space and he guessed there were about 30 pieces inside now; he had not counted. The designer of the Minnesota Flattop, Nils Lou, was in Oregon from his Midwest home early in the summer and helped build this unit during a workshop. Propane-fired, it had sand-colored bricks upon a steel superstructure, and employed a forced-air downdraft damper at the bottom, which meant the gas and flames shot up from the base and came back down again. Pots were stacked on a cart, which was on rails, outside the kiln, then rolled in. The rear end of the cart had a door-like construction that closed the kiln when the cart was completely inside.

Coleman said that if he had bought the kiln prefabricated it might have cost as much as $10,000. He, Lou, Tibbs and a couple of other friends took less than one day to construct it at a cost of about $1,500. Silicon carbide shelves cost an additional $1,200.

In mid-evening, with jets of flame spurting out nearly a foot as he pulled a brick to look inside, Coleman said cone No. 10 was nearly down; the pyrometer read 2350° F. He switched off the heat and said, "We'll open her tomorrow; all we can do now is wait."

At dinner I mentioned having read Susanna Kuo's critique and expressed the view that despite certain critical points she had said much that was positive and encouraging.

"Sure, okay," Tom said, "that's probably true, but it still upset me—the worst of all were those phone calls from potters using the review to get at me."

He had mentioned that several times now and I remarked that I had gotten the impression that some potters were getting at each other all the time anyway. He had talked about that, said he even enjoyed some of it—there was a kind of game with competitive potting, hassling, gossiping and so forth; with talk of who's on top—"You're the best now,"—"So-and-so has slipped, he used to be No. 1,"—"What's the matter with Whatshisname?"

"Yeah, true," Tom said. "It just happens. But apart from that and the phone calls, I've been thinking about that review quite a bit lately—don't know why. And you know what, I guess I'm even changing my work because of it . . . just in the last couple of weeks. Don't know how much difference it'll make, have to wait and see."

It had been only a week or so earlier that he had insisted the review would not change his work for Seattle—"No way," he had said. When I pointed this out now he shrugged and laughed.

There was also some concerned discussion about the printer's continuing failure to finish the flyer. It had been delayed again, neither the Colemans nor Tibbses had seen a proof, and it was already due in Seattle.

September 23, Canby—Tom was fussing around the studio when I arrived, muttering that he had hardly slept the previous night, or the night before—"and when I do sleep I dream about these damned pots!"

From the kiln came muffled hissing and pinging and tinging sound—the pots stretching and crackling as clay and glazes cooled. Tom said the temperature had dropped to 1200° by 7 a.m. and now, 2:40 p.m., was 500 degrees. He unsealed the door, grabbed a flashlight and pulled the trolley cart out seven or eight inches. He peeked inside, flashlight beam cutting the hot darkness.

"Heyyy, oh heyyyy...oh-mi-God, look at that!" he yelled. "That celadon bowl...the tall vase...ohhhhh...all right!"

Coleman's head bobbed up and down from shelf to shelf, eyes opening wider and wider. "Lookin' good!" he called out, then added cautiously, "but that's just a couple of 'em so far, though. Whew! Oh, I can't wait to get this thing really open!"

He paced around, in and out of the studio, ate peanuts, talked and laughed for another 10 minutes. Then he pulled the trolley out about three feet on its rails and darted from one side of it to the other, climbing a stool to see deeper inside. With the door open, the hissing and pinging was much louder.

By 4:30 p.m. he had pulled the cart nearly all the way out and had glimpsed at least part of every piece, although several were still too hot to handle or too difficult to reach. And he could see that a few, including a large and favored platter, had been lost to cracks or crawling, while the great majority appeared fine—more than fine—excellent.

Having already jumped around for nearly two hours, moaning, mumbling, complaining, exclaiming—Coleman said, "Oh Lord, I've gotta get these outta here to see 'em all...can't be sure 'til you've seen all of 'em—inside, bottom, ohhh, man, look at this!"

He touched a bowl with his bare hand, found it too hot, put on a heavy asbestos glove and raised the piece above eye level to catch a shaft of sunlight. "Yeeeeeah! Look at this rosy flash...too much! Couldn't have planned it better. Kissed right off that jar next to it. Perfecto!" He explained the importance of pot placement on the shelves, the relationship of one to the other and to the flame which shot up the sides of the kiln. While he spoke, he was craning his neck, impatient to see more pots, to get his hands on them.

"Oh, boy-oh-boy! Look here! This red...this red is...it's really, just *the* best damned red I've ever done...and look at the cherries over there—look at *that* red! What incredible color!"

He put the pots down and backed away, came forward again and bobbed and stretched to see in the back rows of pots. "Hey, oh wait a minute...this is...I can't wait anymore. Look at that one there, the flat piece! Is that shadow, or is it...? Is that a crack? No, I don't think so; nope, definitely not. And here, this one—*this-one-came-out*! Ohmigod, it's perfect...too much...*mucho grande, signor!*"

His face was flushed and eyes were shining as he brought himself under control and said, "Okay, that's it for now...bad luck to look too long—not yet done. Wait until they're finished."

Coleman pushed the trolley back inside the kiln, closing it completely. He shook his head as we walked into the other room and said, "Whew, that was some load. I have never done a load of porcelain so big, so many pieces at once. Gawd! Think of the hours of work in there. Man, I tell you I didn't sleep all night—not a bit; laid there thinking about this kiln. I got up, came out here so damned keyed up I worked like a madman—over-dosed on tension or something—and decorated more pots in one day than ever in my life. Goin' crazy!"

A smile appeared but was quickly replaced by a frown. "Gotta be careful," he said. "Still haven't seen 'em all. Could still have something go wrong, too. Not time to be so happy yet; too soon, shouldn't be so happy. Take it easy...take your time, dumpkopf, you vant der lightning to shtrike und vanish der potz?"

The hissing and pinging continued and I asked about crackling. He said that "crazing" usually occurred when the clay body did not shrink as much as the glaze. He also explained that potters called it "crazing"—crackling was a "commoner's term."

Babbling with delight, he was not disturbed by the pieces lost in the firing and said that such a high percentage appeared to have succeeded that he could not be upset. In fact, he added, he had felt more disturbed that morning when a nearly 40-inch-high pot broke in the bisque kiln. He showed me the pieces and said, "I really liked that pot, biggest one I ever made...oh well, sometimes you just lose 'em—hope you don't lose a lot. I just wish some people realized how hard this is. *They just don't realize.*"

This somehow got us talking again about the Kuo review and he sounded stern in his rejection of it, compared to his more compatible remarks of the night before. I asked why he was still so upset; what bothered him so much?

The big problem, he said, was that after 10 years of work this was the only written review he had received in his hometown. He had had reviews in several other places, but none here. In fact, potters rarely got full-blown reviews here. Press coverage of their shows was usually confined to brief mentions in roundups of art news or buried in lists of weekend cultural events.

"So, after all this time, we get reviewed, and what do we get? Now don't get me wrong—*Willamette Week* has just started this reviewing and it's great, there should be more of it; I'm just sorry this one was so negative toward me."

I said I did not think it was so negative.

"Oh no, it only said that I don't take my work seriously...and although I've been throwing porcelain for years, she complains that my stuff looks like it was easy for me to do. It's *supposed* to look easy—but it's very, very hard; took years to do it. But looking easy—that's the whole point."

Still excited over the opening of the kiln, Coleman rambled on about the review, disclosing now that it may have helped him in the long run. "You know, it made me think about certain things. All the variety and decoration...well, it's true, I just can't seem to let a side go—I decorate the damned thing—both sides—I decorate 'em both."

But decorating was what he liked most, wasn't it?

"Yeah, that's right—but I have to control it more."

I asked what he thought about the review's suggestion that making pots for sale might rule them out as art.

"Maybe. But you know some of those pots were—*some*—were art. Oh yes, some were, more than a couple were. Were what? Hell, who knows? Aw, who knows!? What's art!? Who says what is *art* and what is *just for sale*? I sweated over that show. Some people liked it so much they came back again and again; lots got in touch with us—we never had so much mail and comment. But some people were teed off because we sold out almost everything; the gallery took in something like $7,000—and some people try to make you feel that is shameful or something. They don't sell their stuff, so they try to make those who do sell feel as if something is wrong, that to sell is a copout."

The conversation ran on for nearly an hour, until we returned to the kiln shed and he pulled the cart completely out of the kiln. Now *I* was excited. Earlier, as the pots were exposed little by little, I was so concerned with problems of photographing Coleman moving around in difficult changing light that I missed the full impact of the pots. And now the sudden full exposure of the cart full of pots dramatized their transformation. The dull glazes and decorations had become brilliantly gleaming colors. Lights glistened and colors flashed in the tiers of pottery as in a mound of precious stones. Some pieces seemed to leap from the stack, others shimmered softly against the yellow-brown shelves and bricks. The profusion of colors was dazzling—celadon greens, several reds, azure and royal blues, creamy whites, sunny yellows...pink!

Elaine returned from the city to pick up stoneware for the ArtQuake booth and looked over the pots with Tom, who seemed much calmer now. He selected a piece, inspected it thoroughly, returned it to the shelf and took another piece—turned it over, held it to the light, rubbed it. He repeated this again and again, saying little, working methodically.

I asked if they felt this was a particularly good kiln load, confessing that I was overwhelmed, never having seen anything to equal it.

"It is very good, really," Tom said almost somberly.

"But you seem so cool about it now," I said.

"He's thinking," Elaine answered with a smile. "He always gets like this after the first excitement. But you're happy about it—right, Tom? See—sure he is."

Coleman grinned and said that he was happy but that there was a lot of work left, this was just the first kiln load, at least two more to go. "I've got to say, though, that I'm really pleased—and surprised—about the red . . . and the red flashes. They are fine. I wonder if that came mostly from the clay? Nope, I bet it's this big kiln—this size is superior for colors, glazes; the gasses expand and expand, work and work in there—and wow."

As he continued checking the pieces he asked Elaine for her opinion about this piece or that one. She was packing stoneware items stored in the kiln room for ArtQuake, and each time Tom called out she looked up, gave her opinion and returned to work.

Little was said about her pots, but Tom gave her a hug a couple of times when what had appeared to be a perfect piece was found to have a crack or glaze crawl that made it worthless. "Bust it . . . bust it," was all she said after discovering the fault in a double-walled celadon box that had been extremely time-consuming and difficult to make. At first glance it had looked gorgeous.

After Elaine left, Tom said he felt very badly about her poor luck in this load. "It's hard to say why. Damn—her best pieces didn't make it. Don't know if the clay was too thick, my glazes wrong—maybe just bad luck." He said two of them might be saved by refiring; they would try.

Overall, however, the results were highly impressive. Tom's favorite pieces included several with ash glazes. One was a large platter decorated with short, curving slip trails that nearly covered the platter's face and formed a swirling sun and cornfield. "My Van Gogh plate," Coleman said.

A large jar had stalks of golden grain and a white sun on a soft blue background; others had flowers, fruit, leaves, abstract designs and motifs reminiscent of Japanese Imari ware.

We counted 40 pots on the cart and probably missed a few small ones in the center. Coleman reckoned that about 85% were up to exhibition standards.

September 23-25, Portland—Coleman reported that the Friday evening opening of ArtQuake was miserable—rain poured down, traffic was hopelessly congested, and the Coleman-Tibbs receipts totalled about $50, barely enough to pay their travel and food costs. The next day, however, the rain slacked off, the turnout improved, and sales picked up. By Sunday evening each couple had grossed about $700 and had enjoyed the fair and friends.

They were not happy, however, to learn that a mix-up with the printed envelopes for the Seattle flyers had caused them to remain at the print-shop all weekend when they should have gone to the Seattle gallery to be addressed.

September 26, Canby—The Colemans returned to the studio this Monday and had to report the most recent problem with the flyers to the Seattle gallery staff. Tom said the gallery people were "very annoyed" over this latest delay because it was nearly the deadline for sending mail to outlying areas in time for the show. These out-of-towners included many persons in the San Juan Islands and other places who were among the area's most avid pottery collectors.

Tom was concerned but seemed unable to get action on the flyer. The printer and designer always had some excuse, which he grumbled about but accepted, partly because they were friends of his and mostly because his real interest was in the pots, not in these peripheral matters. A sharp businessman, of course, would not have tolerated such a threat to sales.

This brought up the general subject of business and administration and how Tom had done with apprentices and partners; he had tried both more than once, but each time something went wrong.

"I'm to blame mostly," he said as he searched through a jar for a certain brush. "I really am, and I know it. I guess I'm difficult—*too* particular. Something always happens. The last apprentice I tried started out fine. He was bright, had a good feel for pottery, everything was right—but it went bad. Little things started it; you know—he was always late, for instance, and I'm punctual, almost always on time, Elaine is, too. So when we were supposed to load the kiln or something and he always came late, it bugged me. Then we had a sale out here and Elaine and I sold a lot more pots than he did, which teed off his wife; I'm still not sure why. We should have sold more, we had been in business 10 years longer. Anyway, he pulled out, angry, left a big bunch of pots here and part of a kiln, and claimed—at least his wife did—that he got screwed after all the work he had done for me, which consisted of helping put in the big kiln and some carpentry. But the main idea in the first place had been that he got to work here as an *apprentice*—he's supposed to do work, instead he ends up all upset. The parting was not pleasant."

Several previous attempts to have an apprentice had turned out poorly also. I asked why he had kept trying.

"Well, there's something about it, I like to help a guy through the problems—I learn something about it in a different way at the same time he is getting something from it. It's good to help somebody, to see growth and be around the intensity of it. I don't need companionship or support or that kind of thing, but I do like that intensity of somebody working, growing. I don't know, maybe I take this work more seriously than I think. Yeah, I guess it's fairly heavy with me . . . ."

The morning slipped by, Tom lunched on his peanuts and raisins, and continued decorating. Elaine worked too, and there was a steady flow of conversation about pottery, old friends, relatives on both sides of the family. At one point Tom proclaimed that he and Elaine were "misfits, outcasts from the artists' society. We really don't belong somehow—not arty enough, or Bohemian enough, never have been. I mean we've got this farm which is pretty good, and we keep it fairly neat, and we've got cars, TV, clean clothes all the time. Some people are aghast when they see how we live—'Hey, man, bet you even got a teevee in your bedroom'—and we do, too. Thing is, I've always been kind of a misfit. At art school, early sixties, I was just out of the Army and had this short hair and funny straight clothes. Gawd, I tried to grow long hair . . . it got fuzzy, looked silly. I tried a beard, it was so wispy and thin it was ridiculous. And my clothes were never right. Even after a fairly long time I felt odd among all the arty people. The thing was, though, there were some fantastically talented people in the school then. Oh man, some could do anything— painting, pottery, sketching, life drawing, name it—they were so good you couldn't believe it. But, do you know that some of the best just blew it—acid, drugs, I'm not sure what—but they blew all that talent. Lost it! I still see some of 'em; it's like they've got gaps in their minds."

Elaine interrupted once: "Tom, you make it sound like you were a real outcast . . . honey, everybody liked you, they all did—sure they did . . . ."

"Well, maybe, after a while . . . but I always felt a little strange."

He also talked about the unhappiness of being an only child moving from town to town, hotel to hotel, and the splitting up of the family. He spoke of that childhood distress as if it was not so long ago.

Then, while searching for another brush, he brightened and said the man who introduced him to sumi had taught a class in it—all the correct strokes and techniques—and the man always told pottery students: "Okay, now you see pot, so nice, sell for maybe fie dollah. But! You put nice decoration with brush—like so (whisk-whisk, flick-flash). Now pot bring you fitty dollah. Ah ha! So, is good to know, yes? Fitty dollah stead of fie dollah. Okay? You bettah come take my course."

Tom finished the story with a laugh, then focused on a porcelain bottle in front of him. The bottle was about 27 inches tall. Coleman said he was thinking of painting a ming tree on it, in four colors. "Man, the first time I did the ming tree I was ecstatic. It blew my mind—and we sold it for $100. My first $100 pot. That was about 1970; a milestone—$100 for one pot."

It would take him considerably longer than an hour, he said as he arranged brushes and paints. He began with deliberation. The tree developed slowly and steadily from the base, gnarl upon gnarl, leaf upon leaf. Shortly before 5 p.m. (the 4 o'clock quitting time had not been observed for weeks) he said to me, "This is going to take time, you don't want to wait around; it'll be late before this old ming is done."

I waited awhile but eventually had to go home. Tom looked up, waved and grinned. It was an engaging smile, had a kind of natural warmth to it; and there was also that glimmer of something quick and alive—challenging? Or responding? Or what was it? I was never exactly sure what it meant, but it never failed to make an impression and remind me of the wide range and variety of his moods and appearance.

September 27, Canby—Coleman divided his morning between brushing and spraying and dripping oxide designs on bowls, and with air-brushing and glazing a variety of shapes. Elaine carved on covers and bowls and boxes. As usual, all of this was accompanied by interruptions from the phone, dogs, children, me, drop-in neighbors, and friends.

In early afternoon, for no apparent reason, Tom began to mutter, "I can't keep doing shows like this . . . can't keep it up. Just too much . . . you can't keep on year after year, show after show. Trouble is—you can't go back to just the old stuff either; casseroles and tumblers! Aw, what the hell . . . ."

I suggested making different things—ash-glaze toilet bowls, celadon false teeth.

"Ho-ho," he replied in monotone, then perked up: "But that reminds me—did I tell you about the dentist? Elaine, remember the dentist?"

It seemed that their dentist's wife had learned the Colemans made pottery and suggested her husband might accept pots as payment of his bill. The couple came to the studio one afternoon, strolled from room to room, selecting pieces.

"The guy tells me to stop him when he reached $110 worth, which was how much we owed him," Coleman recalled. "I said 'okay, you should have stopped a few minutes ago back in the other room.' You should have seen his face. He didn't know whether to laugh or scream. I said the first two pieces he had picked out were at least 50 dollars each and that was a low price...they were pretty nice little porcelains. Ol' dentist turned red in the face, glared at his wife and couldn't get outside fast enough. The wife took the pots, thanked us and left. We never did see them again...got a new dentist."

We laughed, but Tom went on: "That's typical—this guy couldn't believe a pot could cost as much as one of his fillings. But the point is, I worked as many years as he did learning my craft and I put a lot more time and imagination into each pot than he did in my fillings. But he couldn't see that and didn't care. The trouble is that this happens too much."

He returned to work, proclaiming loudly that he would rather give pots free to people who really liked them than sell them to people like the dentist. Soon his grumbling stopped and he worked silently for nearly an hour. I was photographing elsewhere and glanced over to see him squinting at a porcelain bottle, which he held at arm's length, turning it this way and that. He jumped up, lay the bottle flat on a bed of towels cushioning the wheelhead, while mumbling, barely audibly—"look at that. Just-look-at-that...dammit...oh me, oh my...gee-zus, look there...."

He sat, leaned forward to focus his attention on the bottle, dipped a brush in oxide and poised it over the pot...and suddenly darted it down and across the pot's belly and away in an unbroken movement.

Coleman stared at the dark streak, twisted his head from side to side, made a gurgling-laughing sound and did a little dance, where he sat, elbows flapping against his ribs, feet clapping the floor. "Hoo-wee! Hey now, where you been, baby? Where you been?" he said to the bottle.

He finished painting the bottle, smiled at it, and stood it on a table. It had only two marks: a spray-painted circle like a large spreading bruise; a single horizontal stroke that intersected the circle, piercing but not cleaving, so there was fusion rather than division. Another pot beside it had just four marks—a squiggle, a long slant, an arc, and a hazy circle.

Tom picked up an undecorated platter with a smooth, chalky white glaze. I came nearer and he said, "Lookit these! (waving his hand toward the two pieces). It just happens like that . . . see! See that. I *like* it! Damn, it always happens like this—so late. *Too* late, maybe. Hell, I'm almost through. Haw, been working all this time, got all these pots painted, and then whammo, something new comes right through . . . I'm just working away and this design comes straight through at me, and . . . well . . . look at it. Now *that* is something, man. But so late, almost done and here it comes. Still, that's better than not at all."

He studied the platter, nodded and drizzled a line of oxide onto its face. He tipped the plate so the liquid washed down in a wide wave, twisted it so a thin finger streaked far ahead alone, then abruptly leveled the platter, stopping the streak. He grabbed a bottle, shook it, and sprayed a dark brown arc that started and ended on the platter's rim. Several moments passed as he fussed and talked to himself, then dipped a brush and laid it carefully on the plate, the shiny black tip humping up like a small beetle. He drew it across the chalky whiteness about three inches, gave a quick flip and the scarab was gone. A streak of dark oxide gleamed briefly, sank in and turned dull grey.

"Yeah! I like it," he said, "just like that!"

September 29, Canby—The Colemans finished various jobs in the morning with an eye toward loading the kiln in the afternoon. Tom had some large barrel-shaped porcelain jars to glaze by dunking, a difficult job because each one was about 26 inches tall and had to be held under the glaze for at least six seconds against the liquid's upward pressure. The trick was to avoid breaking or cracking the pot.

He glazed several small pots first, easily dipping them in and out of the creamy liquid and sloshing some around inside. Then he put one of the large jars into a barrel of glaze, pushed it down halfway and had to lean on it to submerge all but the mouth. Coleman strained to hold it under, then, with a burst of breath, let it pop up. He timed the surge upward so that at its peak he switched his grip, turned his body, and guided the flying, gleaming pot over to a bench and eased it down.

After repeating this with another jar, he explained that spraying on the glaze was much easier, but dipping into it made a much better surface to paint. Spraying left minuscule bumps, a kind of grainy surface on which brushstrokes had a blurred or bleeding edge, not clean and sharp. And painting on unglazed bisque was unsatisfactory because the clay did not soak up oxides sufficiently, they lay on the surface somewhat as if it was enamel. The ideal finish was plaster-like glaze; it tended to grab at a brush just enough to draw out oxide in sharply defined lines.

Coleman finished glazing by early afternoon and then prepared the kiln and shelves for firing. He loaded the three bottom shelves by fitting small pots around medium-sized pieces with jigsaw-puzzle precision. The upper half of the cart was for the large pots, which towered above a few small bottles and bowls that slipped into open spaces.

Tom would delay lighting the kiln until tonight so that the opening, one-and-a-half days hence, would be in the morning.

In mid-afternoon, a printed copy of the flyer was delivered. It was the first time the Colemans had seen a finished version (Tom had merely turned over the photo and copy to his designer friend) and they were not overly pleased with the pink lettering and type selection, but were glad something was finally being done; printing was to be finished in another day or so.

October 1, Canby—The kiln was expected to be cool enough for opening in mid-morning. Elaine and I made fidgety small talk as we waited and Tom made frequent temperature readings. He was almost grim—like an overly tense actor about to go on stage, a mildly pained expression fixed on his face, a mask that would crack if he laughed. His voice was tight, eyes bright, movements jerky. I asked how he felt.

"Nervous. Heart's pounding," he said matter-of-factly.

Elaine seemed more relaxed, but when Tom finally pulled the kiln door out a few inches and peeked inside, she urged him to hurry up. He fiddled with a latch and she exclaimed, "Oh, dammit, Tom! Open it. Quit teasing—open it!"

But he just shined his flashlight around inside and tipped his head sideways so both eyes could see through the narrow opening. Then his voice echoed back from the chamber—"Oh-oh, damn...looks like we blew it...yep, pretty ba...."

"Com'on Tom, are you serious?" Elaine demanded. "Open it up. C'mon...now!"

He pulled the trolley cart out at least three feet and in the grey morning light pots glistened. The first piece picked up was a stunning double-walled celadon box of Elaine's. Its lines were strong and the color perfect—a softly lustrous green with delicately rich tone. But an inside corner had a short white scar where the glaze had crawled; box ruined.

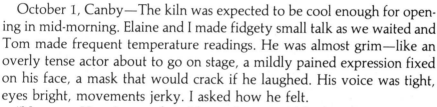

It was just the start. Four more of Elaine's best pieces were lost, including a blue and black box with a wax resist design reminiscent of a woodcut that was perfect except for a streak of dark blue cobalt oxide that had strayed across the lid.

Tom picked up his largest platter—one side had a warp like a fedora's turned-down brim. Another large plate, with a design in brown ash glaze swirling around a green center, also was ruined by warp; a basketball-shaped apple green lidded jar with a rosy blush on one side had two white streaks where the glaze pulled away. And still another large bowl was declared so ugly a blend of colors it would be smashed.

But all this bad news came quickly; thereafter, piece after piece was found without blemish. Perhaps 25 pots had glazing and colors of superb quality. For sheer dazzlement, the prize went to a ginger jar—26 inches high, about 30 inches around the belly—which had the wide belt of brown-purple-pink roots and earth with black gnarled trees and golden sun.

Yips of joy followed muttered curses in the hour-long inspection of the pots. There was much disappointment again for Elaine; of the nine pieces she had in the kiln, six were damaged. Still, she said nothing negative, but seemed to close part of herself off, leaving the rest to enjoy the successful portion of the firing.

Tom's nervousness had faded as soon as the kiln was opened and he got his hands on the pottery. He proceeded with businesslike thoroughness to go over each piece.

That finished, we returned to the front studio where Elaine brought mugs of black Mexican coffee. Tom had a complicated mixture of emotions. He whispered to me how badly he felt for Elaine, but at the same time was looking at some of the best pots he had ever done—"even better than the last firing; it's a little bit overwhelming," he said.

The emotional ups and downs of the morning showed as the Colemans slumped in the studio. Tom's face was flushed with color, his words cascaded out. Elaine sat quietly withdrawn, pensive. Children and dogs came and went as we talked in the smokey-silver light of the foggy autumn afternoon.

Conversation ranged wide and got around to the competition among potters. I asked how it worked, what effects it had, what did it mean? Tom said the competition for respect of fellow potters, for the regard of collectors, gallery-owners and other artists, and for the patronage of buyers were each different but connected to one another. Competition in general was continual and increasing. With other potters, if you had established a reputation you tried to protect it, chiefly with your pots but also with your manners and attitude, your gamesmanship at galleries and shows, and in your dealings with the other potters. The game was going on all the time, whether you played or not.

"I'm competitive," Tom said. "And some people call me a pompous son-of-a-bitch. Now, I don't think I am . . . but, then, maybe I am. Yeah, pompous or arrogant is what I'm often called. And sure I'm competitive. I always have been. To harass you, somebody will call and say—'Hey, man, so-and-so has a fantastic show, the new stuff is just great . . . of course a lot of it looks kind of like your stoneware last spring. Oh yeah, quite a bit—he's really goin' after you, you know that—doin' your shapes, your glazes, your colors. Everybody was talkin' about it. I'd be pretty upset if I was you, man—it was kind of like a parody, know what I mean?' Or people will tell me I'm the top potter around here these days, or that 'everybody says so, man, you're Number One now,' or that the other potters are talking about me, looking up to my work, envious or impressed. Is any of that true? How do I know? I s'pose I hear it quite a bit, though."

"How much is 'quite a bit?' "

"Oh hell, man, I don't know. It sounds ridiculous to even mention it . . . I guess I hear it a lot; different people tell me. Potters will call up after a show with that stuff. Now, whether I believe it or not, there is pressure put on you. Maybe that's why they do it. When they come on with that talk it puts pressure on me I never bargained for. Damn, I don't know, it's hard to explain . . . this competitiveness and pressure is not like you have in a show or entering an exhibit, no, it's more stretched out, goes on and on . . . and it's only with other potters."

I asked if the buying public had much to do with a potter's general reputation and competitive position.

"Buyers can make a difference in certain ways. In some kinds of work, for instance, elite society can make or ruin you because only, say, 10 or 15 percent of pottery buyers can go for the more expensive pieces—and with all the time and energy I put into some stuff I've got to get pretty good prices. So you feel pressure there, different than the pressure you get from other potters. Either way, I guess I just keep competing; keep on driving—want to hold onto my place."

How did that affect him?

It probably contributed to his occasional feelings of being burned out, he said, adding, "I worry about that. Sometimes I think I just can't do this any more. I've got to have a vacation. But somehow I can't take it."

Did he feel a need to be the Number One Potter?

"I don't think there is a Number One Potter. Some serious potters don't even show their work, so how could there be a Number One? Now, as for not showing or selling your work, that's fine for whoever does it, but I can't do that. I've got to sell—not only do I need the money, I want the feedback; I like it, I need it. I get a huge laugh out of people who go around saying that if they didn't have to earn a living they'd just make pots for themselves and that's all—just make pots, look at 'em, break 'em, make more pots...naw, that's weird to me. Now you've asked me if I'm ever going to sit down and make some really far-out pots just for myself...look, I can't even think of that without getting some immediate down feelings. Sure, of course I'd like to make my own pots—I might take a year to make only a couple of pieces, who knows—but how would I feed the family, pay the bills? I guess some people can just push those things aside somehow, but I can't."

What about all the grants, federal assistance to artists, and so on that we hear so much about?

"Of course I've tried for those. A couple of times the slides I submitted to show my work were considered not good enough; another time I didn't fill out a form right and messed up the proposal somehow, some damned thing. I'm trying for a couple more now; I'm told I've got a good chance. We'll see."

We had discussed internationally known potters several times, and Tom's list of favorites included David Leach, Shoji Hamada, David Shaner and Bob Sperry. I asked who he respected the most among the local potters.

"I'd have to say that at this moment I have the most respect for the work of Wally Schwab and Pat Horsley. It's not just that I like their pots, but I also know how serious they are, how much they care about pots. They really love to work with the clay. That's important, and you don't see as much of that as you would think. Some people put the work totally on a money basis—bucks are everything."

Coleman sat on the edge of a table, fingering his mug of coffee and lost in thought, then he added: "I think I respect Pat Horsley in general more than anybody. He seems to live with ups and downs and is fine. I can't do that. I guess he's the nice guy I could never be. He does his work, takes good care of his family—he's got no ego problems. And he does it all so well. I've got such guilt feelings about my family. I don't know exactly...I wonder if an artist should be married? Elaine and I have a great thing, but it's such a selfish thing to be an artist. Sometimes I could cry when my kids want to do this or that and I'm always saying, 'later, later.' I feel so guilty. Art must be the most selfish thing you can do—it takes all your time, all your energy."

The winding down from the kiln opening continued through a fresh pot of coffee. Elaine came in and out. During one of her absences Tom opened the bisque kiln to remove some pots and discovered one of her largest and most elaborately carved bowls had cracks in the lid and the bottom. "Dammit! My fault," Tom said angrily. "I must have got it too hot. Awful!"

When Elaine returned he said "I'm sorry" as he put the bowl before her on the table where she sat. She looked at the piece and with a sweep of her arm knocked it to the floor where it smashed into a dozen pieces. She said nothing.

Conversation lapsed, but got going again before long. Tom said he could not work with anyone for long periods except Elaine—somehow, despite the highs and lows, they came through together okay.

October 3, Portland—I met this morning with Susanna Kuo to discuss her review that had bothered Coleman for so long. She and her husband, who is on the faculty of Portland State University, and their infant son lived on the edge of the city in a lightly wooded area. Susanna's studio for making resist-dyed textiles was in the back of the house; in the living room, where we met, were handsome raku and stoneware pots among other craft and art pieces. Susanna has one sister who is a professional potter and ceramic sculptor and another who is a graphic designer. Her own introduction to textiles had come in Japan, where she was visiting after receiving her doctorate in English literature.

I explained my interest in Tom Coleman and she smiled, saying, "He probably is not speaking to me...he's not a close friend, which is probably good because it's very hard to write a review about someone you are close to; it affects me, I'm kinder, I can't help it."

She expressed the wish for more published criticism of local arts and crafts. "There must be feedback in print. It is much harder, tougher to comment in print, but artists need it—and the community needs it if it wants to develop as an art community. And we must have a variety of opinions, not just mine or a few others; more persons should get involved."

When the talk returned to Coleman, she said, "Everyone admires and acknowledges his technical excellence with porcelain. It is very plastic; his forms are beautiful, very elegant. But I was disappointed in this show—he's capable of more, so I demand more of him. Also, he should edit what he shows; there should have been fewer pieces. I would like to have seen more restraint in the work itself also."

Coleman told me he had removed several pieces before the show opened and I mentioned this now. Kuo said she knew that, but that he should have removed more—"His reputation is pretty well established, he can afford to demand a little more from his viewers, can be more austere."

In connection with sales, she said she fully understood the necessity for selling the pots but asked why, if Coleman wanted to include many pots for that purpose, did he not display them in the sales section of the gallery so the exhibit space would be less crowded.

"And I hope I'm not being unrealistically hard on him," she said, seeming to pick her words with care, "but when I look at that Oriental brushwork I wonder if he is so facile and has done it so easily that he hasn't struggled to produce his own expression."

I tried not to be or sound defensive in his behalf, but said that from all my observations he was thoroughly serious, determined, and hardworking.

"Oh yes, I understand he works hard; and he is so prolific—turns out so many flawless pots—but I'm somehow a little bothered by the Japanese or Oriental tradition being so strong in his work. Now bamboo (a motif on several pots in the show) is fine, but it is not a fact of daily life in Oregon or the Pacific Northwest as it is in Japan or Asia. Why don't some aspects of Northwest life appear on his pots? Use less from the classic tradition and more from the unique aspects of this environment."

In regard to his wide variety of designs and shapes, I mentioned that he had said his shows had a retrospective aspect, some pots represented past phases of his career. Susanna frowned and said she did not understand. I explained and she seemed amazed. "It's almost stunning," she exclaimed, "to think that he can reach back and sort of 'do one' from the past like that. I never heard of anyone doing such a thing; it would be like rewriting a poem you had done five years ago. Hmmm. Almost strange—how could someone just go back like that and redo it . . . and why would they want to, even if they could? I'm surprised to hear about that."

I was surprised that she was surprised; it had not seemed so odd or extraordinary to me. I had quite liked the idea, but, admittedly, had not thought it through. I also quite liked her open and thoughtful responses, and asked for amplification of her references in the review to Coleman's "restlessness" and his seduction by "attractive ready-made images." Kuo, explaining that she had been concerned by the seeming ease with which he turned out such a wide variety of pots, wondered aloud if Coleman ever became so deeply involved in one thing that he fully devoted himself to investigating it, capturing it, putting it into his pottery. "It was that search, that exploring that I missed in the work," she said earnestly, "the sense that there was something he had fallen in love with and was groping to express...understand...share...."

Was there any doubt of his deep involvement in potting? I asked. He had devoted many years, his entire working career, to it—so much so that he feared burning himself out.

She nodded sympathetically. "Maybe he's saturated," she said, "has too much contact with his work. I don't know how anyone can stay exposed week after week without getting kind of sick of their work—you need an empty space every now and then."

Susanna had to be concerned about that in her own work, which we discussed. She was preparing for a show the next month and each piece took days and sometimes weeks to do, depending on its size and complexity. Because the commitment of time and energy could be considerable on a piece, she usually thought each one through thoroughly before starting the actual work. Planning was also encouraged because her materials, such as silk, were expensive.

Returning to Coleman's work before I left, we discussed briefly his artistic development and possible future. "Given his talents and natural predilections—he is so good with the brush, too—it bothers me that he won't, or apparently hasn't, abandoned himself to the struggle," she said. "It all seems so easy, so smooth for him—the porcelain, the brushwork. Where's the true grit? Yes, that's what concerns me. His work is so romantic, so lush—creeping grape vines...cherries...lushness...richness. But when will it get to be more? I don't know, perhaps with his gifts it's a temptation to be a virtuoso, maybe that's what bothers me a bit. I want to see that more personal struggle...."

The interview impressed me with Susanna Kuo's seriousness, sincerity and intelligence. I understood better now her appeals for more restraint and for a particularized dedication or struggle. I still felt, however, that Coleman's variety and exuberance were part of his growing; and his small retrospectives in each show made clear that he was aware and eager to grow. Maturity took time. Also, as in her review, Kuo espoused an ideal—to abandon oneself to a true grit struggle for an artistic goal. But Coleman's self-expression was joined to a family and making a living and to the competitiveness of the potting world. Each of these put limitations on abandonment.

We did not go over all this when I saw Tom at his studio that afternoon, but I did describe my meeting with Susanna and passed along most of her comments.

Tom listened attentively, nodding from time to time, and said he was coming around to a fuller acceptance of some of her assertions, particularly that he decorated excessively and showed too many pieces and too wide a variety of forms and designs. He did not agree, however, that his work had no unifying elements or themes, or that his decorations were overly Oriental.

"No, not too Oriental," he said. "Many have no connection with bamboo or Asia. I mean just look around—right here, these pots—Queen Anne's lace (a jar and a covered bowl had just been decorated with the lace). Now that stuff is right by my back door. It grows all around us here. What about that? Or the Oregon grape? How about the abstractions? Who says they are Oriental?"

As for her surprise over his making pieces representing past phases of his work, Tom blinked and frowned. "What's wrong with that?" he said. "I do that so I can recall where I've been, to remember and reuse the techniques and tools so I won't forget them. That's not bad."

When I tried to describe her idea that his work was so easy to look at that it was not arresting, and that it lacked the evidence of a personal struggle, he interrupted me. "I just don't get that," he said with a shake of his head. "One of the goals is that it *should* look easy. Of course I have to struggle, but that's not what I'm trying to show—it's *supposed* to look easy."

While this struck me as valid, it did not come to terms with Kuo's contention that Coleman's work lacked the "true grit" of artistic struggle. By now, however, I was learning that struggle was in the eye of the beholder. And when it came to describing certain aspects of artwork, perhaps only poets should even try—otherwise, let the art speak for itself.

October 4, Canby—The third and last firing had been completed and 160 pieces of pottery filled shelves and a quarter of the floor in the former sales gallery. Sunlight streamed in several windows and glanced off the pots, making it seem as if rainbows were colliding and splashing color about the room.

Coleman stood in the middle of it, Elaine beside him with a clipboard. He said loudly, "Dammit, I hate this most of all. I don't know what price to put on this thing. Elaine! What do you say? How much? What'd we charge for that little round jar last year at Cannon Beach—you know the one, looked like this?"

"I forget," she said, nibbling at a pencil.

"Oh, hell, nobody knows how to price this stuff—nobody. It's just a wild guess; so what you gonna do, you can't win anyway. I can hear it now—(little old lady's voice) 'But Mr. Coleman I don't understand . . . this nice red one costs more but it's smaller than the green one . . . .' Oh-geeee-zus, how much?"

They had been doing this about one-half hour by now and he was fidgeting and spinning around and hitching up his pants and scratching his head and making faces at me.

"Okay, all right, let's get serious . . . how much for this fat jar?"

Both of them pursed their lips, grimaced, sighed, mumbled. Tom said, "Elaine, now you better decide, you better do it quick, because I am going craaaaazy! How much? Thirty-five . . . Forty-five . . . seventy-five!? I'm sick of these damned pots."

"Now, Tom. Damn it anyway, we've just got to keep at this 'til it's done. No way I'm going to do this by myself; now, c'mon, we'll be here all day at this rate."

They settled down for about 20 minutes of sustained pricing and got through about 25 pots. Then Tom blanked out again. "I know what they *should* be priced," he moaned, "but to look at all of them at once makes me want to vomit. I tell you some of these are worth ten times what they'll ever get! That is true. I mean, I *know* what went into them. But if I put the true price on 'em—well, hell, I'd outrage those people; they'd look at the price tag and walk out. (Laughter) Still . . . we gotta make ourselves a little bread here, right?"

After a few minutes break they resumed pricing. The morning and early afternoon passed in this manner, with one especially long time out while I photographed all the pots together and then again with Tom and Elaine, which were the first posed shots we had done. Then we set up floodlights and put cameras on tripods for color pictures of individual pieces against different cloth backdrops. It was difficult to photograph the finished pots because they were so glasseous, like curving multi-colored mirrors that reflected everything around the room. I would have to experiment with films and lighting arrangements before I could successfully photograph the porcelain in color.

By 4 p.m. the Colemans had selected and priced 96 pieces to go to Seattle for the show. More pieces would go along for the gallery's sales area and the rest would be held for delivery to Oregon galleries and shops after the Seattle show closed.

The flyers had been finished and delivered to Seattle by the Tibbs' apprentice, but they would not be able to reach some people in time for them to make the opening.

On my way home I dropped Tom at a trailer rental garage where his car was being fitted with a hitch and trailer to transport the pots to Seattle. He would pick me up early the next morning, a Wednesday, and Tibbs would meet us in Seattle that afternoon. Our wives would come up together Friday for the opening.

THE SHOW

October 5, Portland-Seattle—Coleman came for me in his 1966 station wagon, which was jammed to the ceiling with boxes of pots. He said that when I had left him at the rental office his car had a hitch and trailer already on it and was pronounced ready to go. He paid and was on the road home when the trailer suddenly gave a violent jerk and careened wildly from side to side, the tongue banging and scraping on the asphalt. Tom pulled to the side of the road, saw that the hitch had fallen off and the trailer was being pulled by a safety chain. He angrily wheeled the car around, filled with thoughts of the likely damage if the pots had been aboard. He dragged the trailer back to its owners, tongue pounding the road, came to a noisy stop outside the office, and instantly everyone was shouting—Tom demanding his money back and the rentors demanding pay for the trailer, whose tongue tip was bent into a U-shape, and the missing hitch. While the proprietors were inspecting the mess, Coleman rushed into the office, grabbed his chargecard rental and deposit slips, ripped them up and drove away with shouts in his ears.

"Every time I thought of what might have happened to the pots I got madder and madder," he said, and by the time he got home he was so upset that Elaine took over. "She told me to take the kids and get out for a while. When we came back she had everything inside the wagon—amazing! I couldn't believe it. I still don't see how she did it—she couldn't have. But here we are...."

Tom's account, punctuated by considerable laughter, got us well started to Seattle. It also set a verbal pace that, keyed up and feeling good, we rarely let lag for the next five hours.

Shortly before 3 p.m. we pulled up to the Northwest Crafts Center, having avoided the guards who try to prevent unauthorized cars from entering the complex of facilities constructed for the Seattle World's Fair and which afterward became the Seattle Center. The Craft Center's several large plate glass front windows looked directly upon a gigantic fountain that changed sprays to the accompaniment of music and lights. Next to this was a grass and stone promenade lined with flags of many countries leading to the Seattle Coliseum, a major sports and entertainment arena.

The Craft Center's staff was expecting Coleman, of course, and greeted him warmly. Manager Ruth Namura was in New York City and due to return Friday for the opening. Shortly after we had carried all the boxes inside, Tom Tibbs pulled up in a van. Within an hour or so all the pots for the show were unwrapped and on the floor. Coleman had his 96, ranging from a three-by-six-inch box of Elaine's to Tom's jars that were two-and-a-half feet tall. Tibbs had about 150 pieces and said his wife would be bringing more Friday. About 50 of the Tibbses' pieces were round closed bottles ranging in size from a yo-yo to a grapefruit; the rest were vases, urns, globes and open bottles mostly six to ten inches tall; a couple of matched pairs may have exceeded a foot in height. All were porcelains with a crystalline glaze—a multi-colored finish notable for enlarged crystal patterns reminiscent of giant snowflakes. I was ignorant of this glaze, so Tibbs gave me a copy of an information card he would be passing out at the opening. It explained how crystalline was produced and concluded by saying that "the difficulties of the process and the beauty of the finished pieces, make these pots among the most highly prized and unusual in the history of ceramics."

Coleman seemed surprised at the number of Tibbs' pots and the two potters exchanged a few mildly sarcastic comments regarding the plan for Tibbs to bring 30 or 40 pieces. Tibbs said it had been so hard to choose among his pots that he brought them all and would let the show's designer decide which ones to display. Coleman suggested that it would be better for Tibbs himself to make the selection because the designer would consider the fact he brought them to mean he wanted to show them. Tibbs said he would wait and see how things went. Coleman told both of us (I would be shooting pictures) to deal carefully with the decorator-designer, who was sensitive and held definite ideas about mounting a show. Tom said he was a professional decorator and designer and set up these exhibits as a favor to Ruth, a longtime friend. Coleman said the designer would arrange the pottery and would listen to suggestions but preferred to be left alone; too much interference might even cause him to walk out. "He's very good, but you must deal with him tactfully and carefully," Coleman said.

The gallery had a large area devoted to displaying craft and art items for sale, including a sizeable selection of pots from many of the better-known Pacific Northwest potters. The show area was even larger. It had one room about 50′×30′ and another room about 20′×30′ with pedestals, boxes, shelves, enclosed counters, and display tables of various sizes and shapes. As we surveyed the area Coleman and Tibbs could not resist asking the women running the gallery what colors had been selected for the walls and when the painters would start work. The women blinked, then smiled and said, "You guys, what're you talking about...you're joking...must be kidding...impossible to paint now...no time." But the potters said it was customary to redo the walls for each new show; such-and-such a gallery and so-and-so always did that. Furthermore, they insisted, the existing wall colors—burnt yellow, smokey orange, muted mossy green—were terrible for the display of porcelain, which they explained with teacherly patience was creamy white and translucent; it would look awful, needed softer, more complementary colors. The women laughed more tentatively and exchanged glances assuring one another that it was a tease.

By this time, however, the potters seemed to have convinced themselves that the present colors were absolutely wrong; worse than that—insulting! "You don't think whatsisname would be treated like this, do you?" They said it was embarrassing; repainting would take only a few hours—why were they being treated like second-class citizens? Start painting this evening and it would be done and dry by tomorrow noon.

The women smiled less and frowned more. They kept insisting there was nothing they could do, Ruth was gone, and besides—"You can't be serious...can you?"

The gallery closed for the day but Coleman and Tibbs kept the subject alive through dinner and beyond, complaining to each other and to me that potters were being treated despicably everywhere, that a painter or sculptor would not be asked to tolerate such indignity—and this was just a part of it, the tip of the iceberg, no telling what slurs would be cast their way tomorrow.

October 6, Seattle—Vern, the designer-decorator, arrived at the gallery in mid-morning. He appeared to be in his 50s, was grey-haired and slim, casually but stylishly dressed, and given to soft, measured speech accentuated with dramatic gestures and an air of slight impatience. I heard painting the walls mentioned to him but once—and then in a sort of half-joking remark that nudged the idea forth tentatively. He responded with a laugh that foreclosed further discussion.

Vern, with an assistant, set to work methodically, studying the pottery and arranging pieces into groups; scooting display cases from place to place; checking lighting facilities. The potters offered suggestions and counsel now and then but it was unclear whether these were having any effect. The only remark I heard from Vern during this period was directed to the assistant: "*All* these pots! My God, I don't know *what* I'm going to do with them." He was informed that the two potters' work was to be kept separate, Coleman in the front main room, Tibbs in the rear, but declared that this was impossible in view of the number and size of the pots. After some muffled conversation, during which Vern rolled his eyes heavenward and sighed audibly, Coleman reported that Vern was a bit annoyed and we had better leave him and his associate to themselves. Coleman, Tibbs and I departed for the rest of the day. Our conversation almost constantly centered around pottery—about making pots or selling them; the competition, the difficulties, the changes in the field. At one point, during a discussion about the lack of standards and how some dealers took advantage of potters, Tibbs shook his head and said determinedly, "Tom, I gotta tell you, you could do a lot more about these things, really. Hey, if I had the power that you do! That's the truth, man, if I had the power and influence that you have—you can dictate, you could get some things done, throw some weight around. You should take stronger stands. It's true. You just don't realize how much strength you have."

Coleman screwed up his face and said something to the effect of that being a lot of talk he had already heard and was not impressed.

October 7, Seattle—The show was opening today at 6 p.m. Coleman was already up when I half-awoke about 7 a.m. I heard him say, "Look, there's only so much you can do—a lot, but only so much. Now as far as I'm concerned all the shapes have been done. Sure, *all* of 'em. They have, that is, if they are . . . were . . . any good; then they've been done because there are no really new forms—nope, all been done for a thousand years."

I made a remark not even coherent to me and Coleman went on: "The fact is, just because all the forms have been done does not mean creativity is shut off by any means. Plenty of room for creativity—*on* the piece, *on* the surface, not *in* its shape. You've got your textures and colors and glazes, your decorations. . . ."

I finally awakened sufficiently to realize he was going through a box of color slides in preparation for the workshop he would be giving. It began with a slide show Saturday evening. On Sunday he would demonstrate and lecture.

Holding up the slides to a lamplight, Coleman inspected and arranged them. He mumbled and laughed, snorted and yelped.

"This is terrible," he said, hands filled with slides, "some of this stuff is just awful...amazing...blimps, I painted blimps. Geez, it's a wonder I didn't know better...whose pots are these? Oh, there's old Creitz (his influence), yeah, these are his pots all right—I made 'em, but they're his pots...Oh, there, now, that's better, more like it—this ash glaze, see here, that's mine; that was important to me...very—then. Whew, this is like going back...seeing ghosts."

When I came out of the shower his attention had turned to potters who did not truly care about pots and only wanted to make money. One in particular irritated Coleman this morning: "God, he makes me sick; sits across the fairway from you and chuckles. Yeah, laughs and counts his money all day. Bundles it up—the money—makes piles of it with crappy pots. Sickening, But what can you do? People don't know what lousy pots those are—he sells 'em a little cheaper than anybody else, people think they got a good deal. They got robbed is what they got."

He was off on something else by the time we joined Tibbs for breakfast and then spent the day going in and out of the gallery. Vern finished setting up in late afternoon, while Coleman and Tibbs were out buying ingredients for the wine punch they would serve that evening.

Then Coleman put on blue jeans newly purchased to replace the dirty ones he wore up, a plaid shirt, and a western-style vest. Despite the onset of a cold and/or allergy attack, he looked fine. His freshly washed hair was glistening and curly, his blue eyes shining, and smile bright as we arrived at the gallery to prepare the punch and put the final touches on the showrooms. They looked fine.

Banks of ceiling spotlights shone with dramatic effect on the grouped pots. The first pieces seen upon entering the showrooms were Coleman's green celadon porcelains—a large platter with a scarlet circle on the face, a two-foot high trumpet vase, a teapot with four cups, a cantaloupe-sized round bottle with tiny neck and mouth. Straight ahead were two lines of Coleman pots—one running the length of the plate glass windows fronting the main room, the other parallel to it on the outside of a half-partition sub-dividing the main room. The window row had clusters of related pots on pedestals and boxy tables; the second row consisted of about a dozen pieces solely in brilliant Chinese red.

On the other side of the half-partition, a four-tiered shelf filled with Tibbs' pots ran the full length of the main room. Against the left end wall were lighted glass cases with Tibbs' round pieces; on the right end were Tibbs' vases and jarlets next to a cluster of Coleman pieces, including his huge favorite ginger jar, which was $500, the highest he had ever priced one pot.

The smaller adjacent showroom had Coleman pieces on pedestals against two walls and on a center table. A lighted glass case against the rear wall contained boxes by Elaine Coleman and Julie Tibbs. Elaine also had several pieces in the front room.

Ruth Namura arrived in the afternoon and welcomed Coleman warmly. He had spoken of her with great fondness and was obviously happy to see her. This would be the fifth show of Coleman's work in this gallery, which she had managed since it began in the early 1960s.

The official opening time was 6 p.m. but old friends and collectors began arriving shortly after 4 o'clock. Even an hour before that, while we were away from the gallery, Coleman's first sale occurred. (Tibbs sold his first piece a day earlier when someone bought the piece featured on his four-color flyer for $250.) Coleman's sale was to a Seattle jeweler who had bought Tom's work for several years and could not come in the evening. He had chosen an ash-glazed platter with a buff-colored base and a charcoal-grey center decorated with slip trails in the form of Queen Anne's lace; it cost $45. A red "sold" dot was stuck on it and caused an early-arriving blonde to wince. She had gone in search of that particular piece, having seen it during unpacking.

"Oh, *that's* the one *I* wanted," she said sadly, and turned to me, the only person handy, to explain that she had bought a Coleman bowl a few years ago and all of her potter friends had admired it as "a potter's pot." She had never met Coleman but when he walked by she stopped him for a brief conversation, and as he left she called after him, "You're a wonder!"

Hearing that as the room began to fill with people and motion, as the pots gleamed and the spotlights beamed, made me realize that this was THE OPENING! Whiffs of show business and gala glamour were faint but present.

New persons were arriving regularly now and Coleman introduced me to a friend who owned an antique shop, then to a potter, then to a painter and his wife. Tom had previously described his pleasures and pains at an opening: He loved the excitement, the bustle and the crowd, the heady and quick conversations with sharp potters and collectors, the competitive gamesmanship and the general feedback on his work. Among his strong dislikes were people who insisted that he pick out his favorite pot or recommend what piece they should buy.

Within the first hour the crowd reached about 100 persons, including several from Oregon who had come north especially for the opening. Red "sold" stickers appeared on seven or eight Coleman pieces.

I found Ruth near her office and asked how everything was going.

"Looks good; fine," she said. "It almost always does when someone like Tom Coleman shows. That's partly because you never know what to expect—it's exciting."

How did she regard this show in terms of Coleman pottery?

"It's even better than I expected—very good, excellent," she said, but her voice was tired. The three-hour time difference from New York and the day's long flight home after a hectic week had left her understandably weary.

About 7:30 p.m. Elaine Coleman arrived with Joyce, and Julia Tibbs. Elaine took a quick stroll through the showrooms—her first look—and went directly back outside to the sales area. She did not appear happy and did not go inside again until after 10 o'clock. I did not discuss it with her but assumed she was bothered by the layout mixing both family's pots together. I supposed also that she was not delighted by Coleman pots being outnumbered in the main showroom; when I later remarked upon this she merely looked at me and smiled.

Tom circulated among visitors throughout the evening, serving punch, telling stories, exchanging gossip and information. The turnout was considered only fair, however; about 500 to 600 persons for the entire evening (1,000 would have been quite good but not overwhelming). More than a dozen professional potters of local note came, including Bob Sperry and Patti Warashina, who were considered to be in the highest rank of Northwest potters and had international reputations.

Concerning the show, Sperry, who taught at the University of Washington, told Coleman that he had not seen so many excellent pots in one place in a long time and asked Tom to give a workshop at the University. Warashina, ebullient and talkative, said it was "beautiful work." Others, such as Ken Stevens and Regnor Reinholdtsen, called it "excellent" or "impressive" or "really great."

It all sounded fine, but what could they be expected to say? Did not good manners dictate politeness, at least? How did you know if they were serious? I asked Sperry and Coleman, who were talking together, how a potter knew if his show was a success.

Sperry pressed his lips together, frowned, then smiled. "Well," he said, "you really know that before the show opens, don't you? I mean you have your own feelings and opinions about the pieces, and what other people say doesn't—or at least it shouldn't—bother you all that much."

Coleman nodded in agreement, then added that "of course, money always has to get in there somewhere, too; sales do count for something."

I wondered how many pots had been sold. I asked Coleman and he said he didn't know and actually didn't care at this point. I said that sounded nice but unbelievable. He shrugged, gave me a testy smile and insisted that he did not give a damn about sales right now because he was much more interested in getting feedback on his work and in talking pottery.

Shortly after that he had a fresh sale and feedback. A shy, but bright-eyed man in his 60s had been going again and again to a bowl of Coleman's. It could be cradled in two cupped hands and was decorated with a burnished gold sun over starkly leafless trees. The man would pick up the bowl, fondle it, turn it over, caress the sides and trace the foot with a finger. He did not appear affluent, but he decided to buy the bowl, which cost $50. He took it to Ruth, who put a red sticker on it and brought him to meet Tom. When Coleman said sincerely that this particular pot was one of his favorites, the old man's eyes sparkled and his cheeks glowed pink. He revealed that he had a considerable collection of pottery, including several of Tom's pieces.

Late in the evening I asked Ruth how sales were going.

"Good...okay, fine, I'd say just fine," she answered. "It hasn't been a huge crowd, but we don't get big openings these days. Seattle has too much competition, too many places to go, things to do. The openings are not like they used to be. And, of course, the flyer was mailed out only a couple of days ago. So...."

I inquired about sales in general and she said the gallery usually made about half of its total at the opening. She added that lateness of the flyer this time meant many persons would come later—"I expect we'll keep selling well for a while. My people—my regulars and collectors—will be coming in over the next month."

Tom talked all evening; with certain potters it was strictly business, with others a lot of friendly joking, and with some a teasing mutual harassment sprinkled with barbs.

I talked with Pat Horsley, the potter friend of the Colemans who, with his wife Arthene, came to the opening from Portland. Pat said he liked the show and that Coleman's work looked good. I mentioned that Tom said he had driven Horsley and Don Sprague crazy during the year the three shared a studio.

"No, it wasn't like that," Horsley said, "not at all. We got along fine, we had no problems with Tom. He's not as nervewracking as he says—at least not by his talking and stuff. I do remember that I got bothered bad one time, though—I was racing him to finish throwing a piece. Thing was, he didn't know I was racing him, so he kept talking and getting up and wandering around, doing this and that...but he still finished first. I was kind of upset about that. I really don't know how he does it—he's just a terrific potter."

Only a few scattered groups came through in the last hour and the gallery closed just after 11 p.m. Most sales appeared to have been made early and I was strongly tempted now to go around the rooms to check each piece to see if it had a "sold" sticker on the bottom.

I did look at some, but felt awkward about it and stopped when I realized Coleman did nothing like that. In fact, I did not see him check a single pot; he continued talking and joking with the last straggling groups of friends. At one point he leaned over to me and whispered, "Failure—a total failure."

"What is? What do you mean?"

"The show...this show—flop!"

He turned away and resumed a conversation and I did not talk to him again until we were preparing to leave. As we gathered odds and ends together I asked him if he really meant the show was a failure.

"Huh? Oh, well, no, not completely...it's just...well, you know, it was kind of a letdown, I guess. Maybe not, but it sure wasn't like that last Portland opening, last spring—whew, man, now *that* was exciting—people actually shoving to get in. I don't know. What did you think?"

I said it was fine, I had enjoyed it, but had to agree that it was not an evening of intense, unabating excitement. The crowd was not breaking down the doors, wrestling for pots.

"Yeah, right...that's what I thought, too. Some really good people came, just not enough of 'em," Coleman said, then turned for a few last words with someone.

Ruth, who was in need of rest, said the show had gone fine and goodnight. About a dozen others of us, including the Colemans, Tibbs, and Horsleys went to a Chinese restaurant, ate and talked until long after midnight. It was pleasant but low key; the climax to months of work found the potters in moderately good humor but too tired or not in the mood for a big celebration.

October 8, Seattle—When Joyce and I checked the Colemans' room to go for breakfast, Tom was already working on his presentation for that evening at Pottery Northwest, the studio sponsoring the workshop. He looked extremely tired and possibly sick. He insisted, however, that he would be all right, and after breakfast we worked together all day on the slide show.

In the early afternoon, Ruth phoned to report that some more pots had been sold, including the large ginger jar—the $500 piece. Although he was pleased he did not seem particularly excited. After hanging up, he merely reported the sale and added that it was nice of the buyer—a Portlander—to come all the way to Seattle.

The slide show went smoothly. Tom showed about 75 photographs of pots he had made in the last 10 years and described various techniques and ideas. The potters paid close attention but said little.

October 9, Seattle—Coleman was pale and congested this morning but opened and conducted the workshop for an attentive, responsive group at the studios of Pottery Northwest. During a break, a woman in her late 20s said she had been following Tom's work since moving west from Vermont several years ago. I asked for her appraisal of his pottery, and she said, "I'm careful of using words like perfection, but his work really does come close to that, I think. It's graceful...pure and clean; varied in its shapes, designs, colors—yet inter-related, too. And it's refined. Overall, I'd say it was *really* excellent."

An older woman nearby overheard us and reported that she had been making pots "an awfully long time," had looked at pottery all over the world, and "read everything ever written about porcelains." In her opinion, "Tom Coleman's pottery is on a par with anything I've seen anywhere."

Coleman threw more than a dozen pots and showed various decorating techniques, including such details as the sumi painting of bamboo leaves which were feathery at the tips, where the wind had whipped them to tatters. The workshop started about 8:30 and was still going at 4 p.m. when Joyce and I left; we had to return to Portland. The Colemans were staying another day or two.

We stopped in at the gallery on our way out of Seattle. Ruth mentioned the purchase of the $500 piece, and said, "We'll sell more over the month, I'm sure it will be good." The pots would stay on display throughout October.

During a last look around, I stood beside an attractive Asian woman in a peach-colored kimono-like dress studying Coleman's red teapot, the one for which he had made a dozen lids before getting a fit. I remarked that I liked the piece and the woman said she was very fond of it and debating whether to buy.

The price ($90) was most reasonable, she said, adding that she had acquired several Coleman pieces over the years. She was still pondering the teapot as we left; I felt certain she would buy it.

Driving home, Joyce and I reflected happily on the weekend and what we thought had been a successful show. I could not resist trying to estimate how the Colemans had fared financially.

The red dots I saw on my last swing around the showrooms indicated that about 16 or 17 Coleman pieces had been sold, with a total value of roughly $1,800.

That sounded fairly good, but we continued calculating. Forty per cent of the gross went to the gallery—subtract $720. For overall expenses we deducted: clay—$150; glazes, oxides, sprays, etc.—$20; flyer—$85; Seattle trip—$200; studio expenses for August/September—$400. These were guesses for the most part, and we tried to be conservative. Our figures totaled $1,575. This gave the Colemans an income so far of $225, or a return of about $110 a month...less than 30c an hour.

The figures surprised us. We went through them again, but came out even more poorly when I remembered that studio expenses should have been higher because he also spent much of July preparing materials and getting ready to make the show pots.*

Of course more pots would be sold, but even if the present number doubled (which was considered the show's likely maximum) it would not produce much income for a family of four. The pots left at home would eventually go on sale, but that would involve additional marketing costs and an unknown amount of time before generating any income.

In sum, then, it looked like it would be quite a while before the Colemans' intensive work for the show earned significant financial returns. We wondered if we had figured it wrong. We must have, it did not make sense. Here was a professional potter who had devoted more than 12 years to perfecting his craft; who had a reputation as technically

*Coleman later reported that my expense estimates were low for clay, decoration materials, and phone-water-electricity by about 50% each. The only item we figured too high was studio insurance—there was none; companies refused to insure it because of the kilns.

and artistically brilliant; who had, together with his talented and able wife, produced the best pots of his life—and it looked as if he would not make enough to pay his house expenses and grocery bills. Had we miscalculated?

October 11, Portland—Coleman, phoning from Canby, said the workshop had been a great success. It ran after 6 p.m., and in the latter stages a convivial mood took over in which he and the potters and students talked candidly about the hard questions of pottery as a career. He said it was unusual that they got down to such realities in a workshop, and he had enjoyed every minute.

In other ways, though, he was not happy. The last day in Seattle had been grey and wet, and the long drive home tiring and cold, he said. Then came a crashing letdown from the opening, the workshop, the months of physical and mental work. Some letdown was inevitable, but this apparently was going beyond what he had expected.

"I don't know," Tom said, "Seattle was great, I really had a great time...but, well, it wasn't so great really. I mean the show was somehow...disappointing. Yeah, and that bothers me because it was the best show I have ever done—really. I know it was my best ever. But Elaine got to figuring last night and we have sold just about $2,000 worth of pots up there. And half a year ago in Portland, we sold $4,400 worth opening night. See what I mean? And we won't see any Seattle money until after the show closes. That means at least next month, and if people pay for pots with credit cards we sometimes don't get the money for months and months. It...it's just, well, I mean what are you supposed to do? Nobody ever said you'd get rich at this business, but, my God! You'd think you could at least make a decent living! After all these years!"

Although Joyce and I had gone through all this earlier I was surprised to hear Tom saying it. I had been expecting him to show me where we had misfigured, but he was confirming that it was as financially depressing as we thought. I mentioned that it had been too bad the flyer went out so late, otherwise the opening might have been a different story.

"Maybe that's right...could be," Tom said, then snorted: "Naw! What's the difference—flyer or not—it didn't make it. I really felt strange up there this time; don't quite know what to think about it. Seattle seems to have changed—really tightened up. And the feedback wasn't that good. Oh, a lot of nice things were said, but there was not enough dialogue or something. Yeah, potters came, some really great people came, but the buyers were not that hip or smart—or even interested. The buyers kept saying things like, 'the pieces are fine, just *so* nice—but a little too high at the moment, a little more than we can afford.' Ruth said she heard the same thing."

I had not realized that this had been commonly said. Many gallery-goers had looked affluent in expensive clothes and jewelry and grooming. I did recall, though, that at least twice, elegantly turned out couples had checked prices on pots—one couple had a $45 bowl, the other picked up a $60 jar—and in each case the partners exchanged "look-at-that-price" grimaces. Merely the accessories they wore cost many times those amounts.

When I mentioned this to Tom on the phone he gave a quick unamused laugh and said, "Right, what's new? Aw, forget the show, I'm going to, got too many things to do." He said he was going to work on the article for *Studio Potter*, clean up his studio, and do some long overdue work on the house—no potting for a week. And he concluded by insisting that he had a good time in Seattle—"The best part was that workshop. It really got going that last couple of hours. The warmth was good; everyone talked about their pottery problems. You know, I think maybe I helped somebody in that session. Hope so. The workshop left me with a fantastic feeling—great, I loved it. Some good people there."

No matter what he said, I remained stuck on the financial problem. Seeing it firsthand had much greater impact than hearing Tom talk about it these past weeks. I wondered how many artists and craftsmen of unusual talent had the same difficulties, or worse.

Kuo made a point when she quoted Ernst Gombrich in saying that only when there is an informed, appreciative and discriminating public "do you get an artist who finds it worthwhile to develop his talents and to improve his styles." I trust that finding it "worthwhile" included enough to buy groceries and pay the rent.

THE UNCERTAINTY

My documentation of Tom Coleman and his work had reached its originally intended end—a pot-making cycle had been completed, the show had opened. But as always in life, endings became beginnings.

What of Coleman's future? What would be the course of his potting and personal development? Would he continue to grow and mature? Or would the financial and competitive sales pressures hold him back? Impressed with his ability and determination, I was also concerned by his self-professed fear of "burning out"—was that a real and imminent danger? Or was it temporary weariness and disgruntlement? And what about Elaine's considerable abilities? And how typical was Coleman, were the Colemans, of potters in general? The answers to many of these questions would take too long for me to answer. In the short run, however, I would see how the Seattle show ended, less than a month away, and meantime there were several persons I hoped to talk with.

Among them was Bill Creitz, back in Oregon from California and something of a mystery man these days. Many theories were expounded for his return and change in direction. Some said he had worn himself out doing a high volume of work; others said he could no longer handle the frenetic California scene, or the breakup of his marriage; still other views were that times had changed, the pottery market changed, and Creitz had either not changed with it or changed too much. The list of possibilities grew with each person who knew Creitz.

He was reported nowadays to be making rough pots on open wood fires, talking mystically, and living in a single room with bed, books, pots and cookstove next to his studio and kiln at George Wright's pottery and clay manufacturing works near Manning, some 50 miles southwest of Portland.

Coleman had spoken often of how influential Creitz had been on his early work and how Creitz had once accused him of plagiarism—"I was shocked; he told me I was simply stealing his ideas—his slip trails, his cylinders. I felt absolutely lost...it was so sudden and final. I nearly panicked."

Coleman arranged a meeting and I drove out October 18 to Creitz's place at the edge of fir woods. It was late morning and he was standing in the door as I came around a hilly bend in the winding dirt road that led to the studio and Wright's pottery.

Creitz showed me his studio and wood-fired kiln inside it; a partly constructed circular beehive salt-kiln outside, which he had been working on for a year; and several boxes of his recent pots. We then sat in his loosely kept, single room with strong black coffee and talked, which Creitz made an earnest and adventurous endeavor. I ran off questions in ones and in batches, and he ran back answers and opinions on them and anything else that came to mind in double batches. This went on for two or three hours. Some of the highlights:

About earning a living, Creitz said it was virtually impossible to sustain a high living standard as strictly a potter—"Teaching, though, is deadening!" The most famous contemporary potters had difficulties, he said. "Even Voulkos can't make a living just making pots. Oh, sure, you can do it for a while—even a few years; I did it for four years; made fifty-thousand bucks a year—for four years! But then it goes. You use up your energy. Take a look at others who were big once, making the big money, they burned, lost it...You get lost in your own ego. Here you are trying to be the best—you know, man, THE BEST! Greatest! The truest! Whatever—and you have got to be competitive, man. Oh yeah, *competitive*! But look what happens...(he stepped to a table, sorted through a stack of magazines and thrust a copy of *Studio Potter* at me). Now just look through *that*, man, you'll see what I mean!"

I turned the pages, which featured many potters talking about their work and their lives; photos showed them in their studios, surrounded by pots and/or families.

"See what I mean?!" Creitz asked. "*Look* at those faces—I mean look, man, at those *faces*! Look at the *resignation*. Oh, yeah—wow; that's what it does to you—all those years; and those faces tell it. Resignation! What kind of life is that?"

He had remained standing, voice and body tensing as he made his point, then he sat again, and said, "Well, I tell you I'm getting back to basics. I've been trying to get it together. Hell, in my big years I was swinging, and that was okay for then—you know, the big cars, living big, the whole California scene, you know; and that was good for me, taught me a lot—but it cost me, too. But I had to go through that, I guess. Now I'm back to working on my craft; I'm trying new stuff again—forms, decorations, lots of different trips. Doing some good stuff, good stuff."

I had seen pots he had made since coming back to Oregon—some were sharply different from his previous work. I did not prefer the new back-to-beginnings pieces with their muddy brown and black colors, crude forms and rough textures. Creitz showed me examples of his older and also his most recent work which I liked. There were cannisters and drum-like boxes and containers in buffs, various darker browns and blues with slip trails in Asian configurations.

"You know," Creitz said in his quick and urgent manner of speaking, "all artists have this problem—you are going along, working with your craft and trying to get someplace; but when you get there—what? You reach it, but then where do you go? Your ego stares back at you. Then you need a new dimension. But what you have to learn—or remember—is that all there really is is silence, darkness, time and energy. That's all...there is...."

The conversation followed these lines for a while, then Creitz said: "Hey, man, I don't even consider myself a potter anymore—no way; no more. I got pots out there—make maybe $200 or $300 a month selling pots—but look, this is no success trip anymore. Naw, making pots now is a meditative experience: a Way."

When I turned the subject toward Coleman, mentioning that he had said Creitz was a major influence in his career—both as a teacher and as a model or inspiration—I recited Tom's story about when Creitz smashed his pots.

"I did?" Creitz responded with a puzzled frown. "I smashed them—really?"

"You mean you didn't?" I said. "Tom says he was working with you, as kind of an apprentice, and after being away somewhere you came back and looked at his pots, said they were terrible and smashed them. He says it was one of the most important and good things that ever happened to him as a potter."

"Oh yeah—right—right! I remember now...but...are you sure he said I *smashed* them? Maybe...I...really...don't remember that exactly. But I do remember the scene, man. Oh, sure."

"What about that? What were some details?"

"Well, I remember that Tom wasn't doing anything. There was this long period of him doing the hokey stuff and I came in—I'd been away in Canada on a teaching job, I think—and I came in and saw *all* these pots, and they were...just...nothing!—*zero!* They were all things he'd seen me do. It was awful. I said so. Hell, man, I wanted to see his mind, his own creative processes—didn't want to see this stuff. I think I even said something like it was plagiarism or something real heavy like that. Anyway, I told him he *had* to come up with something, if he didn't he just would not make it—no way! Then I walked out."

"And what happened?"

"What happened? Oh, hell, man—he *did* it. I mean he very quickly found his own idea; his own style. But the thing about Coleman was that he was a good student—always. Intense! See, he took it as a challenge. He wouldn't be beat. But others? Aw, I had to nurse and baby 'em. Forget 'em, they never made it."

"And what about Coleman's development since then?"

"Good, very good—he is a good potter."

"So, how would you rank him? Where?"

"Well, he's *up* there, you know—he's at the top right now. Really at the top. But that's all relative, you know. That's all ego and competition and I don't really dig that anymore. Now Tom has things to learn. His big weakness is that he is basically so conservative. He wants to go with a sure thing, which means he is always committed to repeat what he's been doing...."

But, I said, Coleman maintained that if a potter expected to make any kind of a living at all, he had to keep making a certain number of things that sold.

"Right. He's right! But that's the whole thing, man, if you got to have money, or you've got to keep a family, stuff like that, well, I don't know...maybe forget it. The whole thing gets to be a question of sacrifice."

"You mean give up everything—families, kids, wife—for the art?"

"Well, what's new?" Creitz said with a crooked smile and ran his hand through his hair. "I mean that's the age-old question, right? Nothing's really changed for centuries. The artist has that problem, always. Guess it's gotta be that way. Same as—oh hell, so many. I just reread *Pierre;* you know, the Melville thing about the pain of being an artist. Oh, man, did he get put down."

"Are you saying that unless Coleman gives up all those things he can't succeed?"

"What do you mean by *succeed?* What I'm saying is that there is a lack of freedom in his work—too much restraint. But then maybe all of us have that problem to a degree. But if Tom could just get rid of all this restraint of his—break loose, let go—my God! There's no telling what he might do. He's got the ability."

I had brought a collection of slides of Coleman's most recent pots and asked Creitz if he would like to see them. He said yes, but declined my offer to set up the screen and projector I had with me; he insisted that he wanted to merely hold them up to the light. He squinted and nodded or frowned as he put each slide up to his eye.

"Say, these are not bad...yeah...that's okay...." He went along in this manner, making comments frequently: "Well, now I don't care much for that;" and "Hey, now, this one's got more freedom, see that carefree quality?; a real change, I like it a *lot*;"—"so that's Elaine's, she's very good."

After he finished looking at more than 100 slides Creitz leaned back in his chair and smiled, rather inwardly and privately. Then the smile broadened to include me—it was a bit cockeyed: Creitz had a slight gap between his front teeth and it gave his grin a disarming quality. Earlier, he had had moments of intense, eyes-flashing zealousness that kept me at a distance, but now he was almost boyishly charming.

"Yeah, I see it's there, man," Creitz said. "He's done some new stuff—Elaine, too; she's really coming along. Yeah, Tom's done some new good stuff—but still, Tom wants respect. He wants it so bad that he can't get it. You just can't do it that way; you can't care too much, you know? You can't be careful, or sure, or just make beautiful pieces—you know? Aw, I mean, what's beautiful? Hell, any number of people can—and do—make beautiful pots, right? But they get successful, and then you always know what the next pot is gonna look like. So...." he grinned and made a palms-up "what-can-you-do" shrug.

We talked about current potters and Creitz categorized them as 1—top producers; 2—purely artists; 3—strictly commercial; 4—Saturday marketers; and 5—hobbyists. I mentioned a rather prominent potter and said his last show had left me cold; his pots were empty lumps, even their grotesqueness was dull.

"Oh no, man, that was *some* show. I'll tell you, that stuff was bad, right? But I mean it was *so* bad, see he was struggling right there in front of you—trying, hurting; man, that takes guts to put something that ugly in front of people. He knows, man, how ugly that stuff is, but he's trying to find a new direction. Not just the same old beautiful pots, okay?"

It was time to leave and I asked where Creitz thought Tom's work might go.

"It's all like I've been saying, man, he's gotta live more fully—live! Get rid of fear and anxiety and he'll go. He's got the potential, but he has got to get rid of the fear and anxiety—I guess a lot of us do. Depends on how bad you want it, and yet *not* want it at the same time. You can't want it *too* much, yet you've got to want it *more than anything*. Right?"

I nodded and shook my head at the same time, then said goodbye. Creitz said he was going to work—"making pots is what I love; just get on that wheel and it never—never—fails to give me a big lift."

The talk with Creitz stuck in my head for days and I asked Coleman later about various points. Tom said he had had similar discussions with Creitz and there was some merit to what he said, but a lot of it seemed to be philosophizing and phrasemaking simply for their own sakes. "That may be fine for some people—but it isn't my style," Coleman said. "I need to do things. I like talking, but I've got to work—at the same time, I guess. And to tell the truth, I can't figure out what Creitz is talking about sometimes...I wonder if he can. Lots of times he just says things to try them out, or to try *you* out—see how you'll react."

Coleman thought a moment, smiled and said, "He's sure right about one thing, though: he has changed, not the same guy who drove the big ol' Lincoln Continental and dressed in cool dude clothes. And hell, he's also right about traveling and having some fresh ideas and stuff...thing is, everytime I look up it costs money; you can't escape it."

Up to this time, virtually everyone I had spoken to liked Coleman's pots, in degrees ranging from dutiful respect to adulation. I wanted to talk with some people who did not like his work. Coleman himself had suggestions. "There's plenty," he said. "You might talk to George Cummings; he was an instructor down at Portland State same time as me. Or how about ol' Horsley, he has never much liked my work."

"You serious? Pat Horsley? I thought he was your good friend."

"Yeah, he is. Pat's the kind of guy who can be your friend like that and never BS you about your work. Oh, he thinks my work is okay, but he's really never much liked my kind of pots—he's always been sort of anti-the-reds, for instance, and a lot of my other work. We just do different stuff, that's all. He's doing production only now, but he has great imagination and artistic ability."

Pat Horsley was working at a wheel beside the front foor of his studio when I arrived, as arranged, the afternoon of October 20. His colleague Don Sprague was away so the wheel on the opposite side of the room sat idle. The studio, in what had been a small store, was narrow and long with storage racks, work tables, mixing benches, packing crates, bins, boxes, equipment and materials neatly occupying all of the 30 feet or so of space between the wheels and a smaller rear room which held kiln, vats, and clay-drying troughs. The kiln, fired just that morning, cast an orange glow and warmth.

Horsley, 34, married, and the father of two children, had been making pots for a living since 1971. He had a thick dark short beard and wore heavy overalls. There was something mature but at the same time youthful in his manner and appearance, and I kept expecting his speech to be with a Welsh or Irish sound. But his American came through the whiskers clear and unencumbered by accent. Nor was there any hip-slang or potters' lingo.

We quickly got into the increasing number of potters in Oregon, which I understood had gone from only a few dozen a decade or so ago to a couple of thousand now.

"True," Horsley said, "why 25 years ago there were probably only a few dozen potters in the whole United States. The growth has been just phenomenal." The results were mixed, he added, because while the greater number of potters made for tougher competition, it also heightened the interest of the buying public and broadened the market for hand-made pots. Sales and marketing became more complex, but with more varied opportunities.

In his approach to the financial problems, Horsley said he worked on a quota that required him to throw and/or finish enough pots each day to earn a gross retail return of $300. From this amount he would pay dealers (an average of 40% of retail price), material and studio expenses, income tax, social security and so forth, and have roughly $90 left as daily net income. This would be realized, however, only on the approximate 20 days out of 30 in which pots were being thrown and finished; Horsley put the other 10 working days into glazing, firing, packing, pricing, mixing clay, and other non-throwing/finishing tasks. Therefore, on the basis of 275 total annual workdays (5.5 days each week for 50 weeks; two weeks off for vacation and illness), the 184 paydays theoretically would produce about $16,550 a year. But, of course, every additional day away from throwing/finishing because of technical problems, supply snafus, illness and other business or family delays reduced income.

Horsley said major problems for a potter making his type of production ware were in getting top display space and art grants. "My stuff is good, I know it, but not new and different. Right now I don't want to do anything different, I just want to make good strong pots. But you're not going to get priority space in galleries with it—they have your work, but down on the bottom shelves. And when it comes to grants, they look at slides—how can they tell quality? But they can tell if the pots are wild or arty, so...sorry."

I asked if he was looking for more business.

"Oh no, not more. I'm selling everything I can make. I can't make any more and maintain quality. We're pushing it out as fast as we can."

Why not raise prices?

"Yeah, well, that's what everybody says—but you know I worked and struggled so darn hard to get my pots into some places that you've got to be careful about raising prices. There are so many potters out there just waiting to get a crack at sales—they sell for less and they want to get in there. Raising prices is taking a risk I don't think I can afford right now. What a few of us have talked about a long time is having our own sales place, our own outlet. Now that would be something if we could make it—keep that 40% for ourselves."

I showed the slides of Coleman's Seattle pots and Horsley saw some new designs and new ideas which he liked and which foretold even more changes ahead that he thought would be good. And he saw a few things he did not like, such as an ash glaze he considered faulty. "I know the ash glazes, do a lot of 'em—Tom's got a little too much thickness in the tip of these dripping edges. See here...."

I mentioned Coleman's statement that Horsley did not like his pots.

"He said that? Aw, that's not true. I like his pots fine...well, I'm not crazy about *some* of them, that's true; but then I could say that about many potters, and they about me."

I mentioned that Coleman had emphasized how much he appreciated the praise Horsley had previously given him about the Seattle show. "He said he liked the praise because it was so rare," I added.

"Oh well, I don't know about what Coleman says," Horsley said, "but you know, he does tend to talk, he really can go on and on sometimes. Actually, one of the most important things about Tom is that he sets standards for potters—and he doesn't even realize it. Now he does very fine porcelain—the best I have ever seen, although admittedly I'm not well traveled. Still, it's the best porcelain in the Northwest, I'd say—could even be best in the country. But that's not what I'm talking about exactly when I say he's important. I mean, for instance, that he taught me concern for perfection. That may sound a little odd, but it is important—even though perfection may seem unnecessary in what I'm doing, which is production stoneware—casseroles, place settings, goblets, cups; you know, the same things over and over. But I try to do each one right; and I know that I do it a certain way probably because of Coleman."

I asked him to be specific.

"How Coleman sets standards? Well, there's such a thing as making lids fit—always! I mean Tom taught me that a lid must always fit—fit properly. A piece can't go out of the studio if it doesn't fit right. You used to see—still can for that matter—casseroles or any kind of pot for sale with a lid that rattled and scraped; or it wobbled and caught in places; wasn't tight all around. Coleman would never allow that. And he taught me that. Same way he made it matter to trim the feet—you must pay attention to the foot of a pot, can't leave it sloppy or uneven or rough—now that takes extra work when you are turning out stuff at the rate I am. To spend a few minutes more on each piece, to do the extra work on just the foot costs you a lot of time and energy and money before you are through. But I've got to do it—Coleman instilled that in me. I'm not sorry, though I sometimes wonder if I haven't gone too far with it."

How did Coleman establish or implement standards?

"Well, I was in his classes for one thing, and so were other people who are potting around here now. But I think he sets the standards more by his work. You never would see a pot of Tom's that was shoddy or sloppy. I mean the piece does what it is supposed to do—in a functional way first of all, but at the same time it is handsome or beautiful or whatever. A teapot must pour properly; it must have balance when it stands and when it is held and tipped; it should not be too heavy and so on—lots of things, some of them small and seeming kind of unimportant, but they *are* important. There are all kinds of people making bad pots, almost anyone can do that. But Coleman establishes an elegance of the pot, an elegance of a teapot, an elegance of any pot he does. Now *that* sets standards."

"And you like his pots?"

"Some. . .I like some a lot."

I left soon after that. Horsley was pulling bricks in the peep holes of his kiln and the white-orange flames were shooting out at his beard. "Looks real good in there," he said.

I was eager to meet also with a woman named Leta Kennedy. Coleman had said that he got into pottery by taking a ceramics course while studying painting. The ceramics teacher had been at the museum art school as long as anyone could remember.

"She taught design basically, but she also taught pots," Tom recalled. "I wasn't so hot for it, but something kept me at it—even though she made you clean glazes off the paper towels and save them for the next class. I nearly went nuts. I wanted to get on the wheel and throw pots so bad, but we'd throw for only one day, then pick one of the pots we made and decorate it for a week. Yep—a whole week. The same pot. We'd put on a slip and etch away, etch away, then glaze for days—on and on. And this little ol' lady teacher Leta Kennedy—how well I still remember her, she had a little problem with one foot and used to eat these tiny sand-wiches—she almost drove me crazy. After I really got turned on to the pots I was always dying to get on the wheel. But we did it her way. And the truth is—and I never realized it then—that little ol' Mizz Kennedy taught me more design than I ever dreamed. Really. She taught me more than anybody. And the stuff came back years later—it *still* comes back. Whew! That was *some* teacher."

Coleman traced her through the museum school (she had retired) and arranged a meeting for us. Tom had not seen her for quite a while and came with me to an hotel-like apartment for the retired.

We knocked on her door about 10:30 a.m. and Leta Kennedy invited us in to take seats on a sofa and an easy chair. While she and Tom recalled school days I half-listened and glanced around her apartment. The main room in which we sat was neatly filled with tasteful older furniture, mementos, several paintings, prints and wall hangings, and tidy stacks of books and papers. I had a sense of all these things having a distinct place in the room, although there was no feeling of fastidiousness or strict order.

Miss Leta Kennedy's eyes were as clear as her slightly olive skin, which was surprisingly taut over a finely-shaped forehead and cheekbones. Her silver-grey hair was pulled straight back and tied behind her head. She was slim, and seemed at once fragile and firm, resilient. She wore rimless eyeglasses and a short-sleeved print dress and black shoes—one with a thicker heel and sole. She was a handsome woman now and I wondered if she was a beauty in her younger days.

She indicated that she was about 80 years old, recalling that she had gone to the Museum Art School after graduating from a Portland high school in 1915. She spent the first three years as a student, served a while as a teacher's assistant, and finally became a full teacher, which she remained until her retirement in 1971.

Her speech had an almost formal clarity, with occasional pauses to find the exact thought or word. She seemed delighted to see Tom and recalled attending his show at Contemporary Crafts in the spring. He was sorry to have missed her and said he had not even known she came—was it at the opening? No, Miss Kennedy said, she did not go out at night anymore and so had taken city buses to go over and back one afternoon—"I go whenever I can. I do like to keep up with what the students are doing."

I wondered how many artists were unaware of her quiet, unobtrusive interest in them. As they talked, Coleman, who had mentioned not seeing her for quite a while realized it had been since his graduation more than a decade ago.

I asked about her approach to teaching art, and Miss Kennedy said she had always directed her work toward the fundamentals—"Design is at the base," she said firmly, adding that she sought never to force ideas on students and wanted them to learn by doing a thing over and over again.

"I always try to take the student as the student is," she said. "Yes, take them as they come to you, try and understand where that is, where they are, and then determine how you can be helpful."

Was there anything she regarded as particularly important in the teaching of art beyond the usual development of techniques, perceptions and so on?

"Well," Miss Kennedy said, stopping momentarily with a finger to her lips, "...I always felt that intuition was very important. And that is hard for some students to realize—they don't know how to realize their intuition. They are too intense to understand themselves. But why be so self-centered, I say. You must relax and let it happen...trust it."

Her sentences came with the even, almost measured rhythm of one concerned that each word was being heard and understood: "But, of course, as a teacher you can only teach a method. Ideas—no; the individual has to develop his own ideas. You can have sympathetic discussions perhaps, but the individual must go alone."

We brought up the difficulties artists had making a living, and wondered how she as a teacher felt about it.

"Oh my, yes, I remember so well how Miss Crocker and Harry Wentz used to worry about the numbers of people going into arts and crafts to try to make a living. It just looked impossible. Of course, I can remember the time when painters around here wouldn't *think* of selling—oh no—they felt there was a stigma attached to selling a piece of artwork." She said the only potters who made real money during times past were those doing technical ceramic work at a local scientific laboratory. She told anecdotes about artists who would sell and those who would not, and how they argued over what was art and what was craft. Then she said:

"But what is art anyway? Croce—Benedetto Croce, the critic and historian—puts it in a certain way and I've always remembered it. Croce said: 'Art is an aspiration...in the circle...of...a...representation.' So, 'Art is an *as*-piration in the circle of a *rep*-resentation.' Hmmm, yes; I've always liked that. You see—vision is not enough, you must do something about it!"

With this she seemed almost back in the classroom—leaning forward in her chair, head up, projecting her thought and repeating it with emphasis on the key words so everybody got it. The presentation was completely natural to her, of course, and the clear diction and disciplined modulations of tone suited the delivery well. Her eyes flickered with excitement as she recalled Croce's idea, shared it, developed it.

When the subject later turned to pottery she felt constrained to say that, frankly and unfortunately, she could not recall Tom's work in her class—however, she quickly added, she remembered him as a person and had followed his career. Tom assured her that he had done nothing memorable in school. Miss Kennedy then remembered Elaine, too, and inquired about her.

Asked if she recalled specific pieces from the Colemans' last show, she said, "Oh, yes, I remember the show well. I was quite interested to see that you are drawing on your pieces. Now that means, of course, that the decorations are not just a happenstance that the kiln does; no, you have used a certain brush for a certain thing. I liked it. And I felt a certain Oriental quality." She added that she approved the decoration of pottery and said history had shown this to be "a perfectly legitimate pursuit." The crucial point was that the decoration belong to that particular piece—otherwise it was detrimental.

We pulled the shades on her wide windows and projected about 100 slides of Tom's recent pots. She commented now and again throughout, apparently enjoying herself and the work, and concluding that the painting and ceramics had worked well together. "It was very competent, very beautiful," she said when I asked if it was possible to sum up her reaction. She singled out several pieces which exhibited influences she described as from the Far East to the Middle East, including Persia.

We asked about her own career as an artist and she inclined her head a moment, then said, "I had intended to be a painter, not a teacher, although even as a student I seemed to be the one asked to help with the class and such things. But over the years I found that I just couldn't teach and work, paint. I tried often and just made myself sick, physically sick; I wasn't up to it."

Tom said that he had the same experience exactly and she nodded sympathetically before going on: "I had been serious, trying to work *so* hard. I had summer programs with Hans Hoffman—oh my, how extraordinary *that* was—and another summer with Mohaly Nagy; ah, another marvelous experience. But, at some point, I just finally said it was all right to be a teacher. I don't recall that it was just a simple clear decision, it just happened and I accepted it. I liked it. I always liked teaching." There was no trace of regret in her voice; she clearly had come to terms with the decision long ago.

The discussion grew nostalgic as she recalled her half century at the museum school and talked with great warmth about certain colleagues, naming many and recalling this or that incident, laughing with pleasure over certain events and idiosyncracies. Then she announced rather strongly that she had frequently felt there was too much monotony in art, that it needed more and more freshness all the time.

Another thing that had frequently impressed her, she said, was that many people who came to the art school would not—or could not—have made their way through general schools: "You'd be surprised how many couldn't write or express themselves well in words but did well in visual expression. I always thought that that was interesting. If they had been in regular schools they probably would have failed or been labeled dull—but in the art school they were fine."

Having stayed more than two hours, it was time to go. Tom told Miss Kennedy how greatly he had come to treasure her teaching; her modest protest did not hide her smile. Saying goodbye, she guided us to the apartment's main door, the inside of which held a sort of bulletin board with calendars, newspaper clippings, notes, souvenirs, snippets and oddments, and a white poster with a single teapot on it over the world "Coleman," the flyer from Tom's show many months earlier.

We teased her lightly about having hung it because Tom was coming to visit; she tsk-tsked and laughed as we left.

Sometime after that I remarked to a friend who formerly taught at the museum school about meeting Leta Kennedy. He beamed. "Hey, you are lucky," he said. "I didn't realize she was still around. Do you know, over the years I've come to the conclusion that Leta Kennedy is probably the single most significant person in the art of this city. That design class she taught—wow, look at all the artists who took it, and used it all their lives: It's all over this town."

A name that came up fairly often in conversations about Oregon pottery was Ray Grimm, head of the department of ceramics at Portland State University. Many of the leading local potters of the past two decades had studied or taught at the school, and Ray, himself a potter of considerable reknown at one time, had seen them all come and go.

Coleman had taught in the department and arranged for me to meet Grimm in his home in Northwest Portland October 25, but when I arrived two of his children said Grimm had just left on his bicycle for his office and would be there in about half an hour.

I drove toward the school, which took me past an area known for its potters, studios, workshops, suppliers, sales rooms, taverns and potters' haunts on or near Northwest Thurman Street. Coleman, Horsley, and Sprague had had their joint studio here a few years ago, and nowadays many persons worked out of the Potter's Workshop & Gallery, where beginners studied and professionals rented space and equipment.

I went into the workshop, saw three women preparing pots for a tall kiln and introduced myself as a journalist interested in pottery. I asked if they would answer some questions. They hesitated, looked at each other and back at me, shaking their heads that they did not much like the idea. I was merely after general information and assured them they could be anonymous if they wished.

"I guess that's okay," said the youngest-looking member of the threesome, a tall brunette in her early 20s. But before I could even get started one of the other women said, "Are you doing a book about Tom Coleman?"

Seeing my surprise, she explained that a potter friend of hers—who knew Coleman and me—had told her someone was doing a book and I seemed to fit the description.

The younger woman said, "Oh, really, a book about Tom Coleman? So, you're a big fan of Coleman's, huh?" She shrugged and frowned in such a way that I could not tell if it signified disdain or indifference, or was simply a mannerism.

The third woman, the oldest, perhaps in her 40s, said, "Oh yeah, that's the *big time*, right? Well, that's really something. What're you doing *here*?

I asked what was wrong. The youngest, who had a kind of street-wise confidence spoke up:

"I'll tell you. It's not all fun and games, you know? It's tough trying to make it and the thing I resent is that there are up-and-coming potters, good potters, damned good potters, who can't get into the galleries and shows. That's right. Couple guys working out of here are really super, really super, but they go to the galleries—including *the* gallery (Contemporary Crafts)—and are juried out. You've got no chance unless you are on the inside with the old crowd. And so you come around asking questions and you're a big fan of Coleman's, and he is really *in* with *the* gallery; heavy in, right?"

The older woman spoke up: "Oh well, I don't think that's the point. I've seen Coleman's stuff—terrific. So what has that got to do with anything here?"

"Oh well, I'm not saying he's not good—I like his stuff, too; but I'll tell you some people don't," said the first woman. "Take Brian—he says Coleman's stuff is dead...no good; says it's just lifeless, dead."

"I think it's wonderful," said the third woman, the quieter one, who had known about the book.

The tougher one replied: "Okay, look, I'm not saying anything—I like it, too—but, I'll tell you this: Did you see his booth at ArtQuake? No? Well, he had mugs with—get this—extruded handles! Oh-mi-god, I couldn't believe it: Exxx-truuuded handles! Gee-zus, The Great Coleman...ha!"

"Well, I don't know anything about that," the older woman said, "but I saw his show last spring and absolutely loved it. The forms were beautiful...."

Switching the subject from Coleman, I asked what it was like to get started as a potter. They all spoke at once. Each had been making pots for three or four years. One wanted it to be a full-time occupation, the other two thought it would never be more than part-time. All three sold their wares at the Saturday Market, a collection of stalls, stands, booths, and kiosks put up every weekend in downtown Portland, at the foot of the Burnside Bridge beside the Willamette River, near a onetime artists' quarter. The Saturday Market had started about 1973 with a few crafts-men, artists and food vendors and caught the public's fancy. Participants originally had just showed up and put out their goods, but the demand for space became so great that it was necessary now to make reservations. The women said that about a half dozen potters had been involved at the start but sometimes lately 30 or more set up on a given Saturday with another 20 wanting space.

How was it working out?

"One of the biggest problems is—let's face it—men are more aggressive than women," said the oldest woman. "We just lose out. It is really hard for me."

"Yeah, I suppose that's right," said the younger one, "but the thing that really gets me is how little you make for all the time you put in—it's ridiculous! It figures out to a buck or less an hour. I sometimes wonder why I do it...really."

"Do you suppose Tom Coleman does a lot better?" I asked.

This brought a chorus of haw-haws and snorts, including some from another woman and a man who had just come to work and were listening in.

"Are you kidding? Coleman?" a woman said. "Ha—he's got it *made*, man. Why, he has got it cold! Can get a show anywhere, can get his stuff into *any* gallery or shop. Don't make me laugh."

"Oh brother," said another, "is he making it? We make *nothing* by comparison."

I tried to say that things might not be as vastly different as they imagined, but they were not convinced by my figures, and continued with what had become a conversation among themselves:

"Well, the hardest part for me is still selling—much harder than making the pots," said the older woman.

"Oh hell, I can sell 'em," said the younger woman, "but what gets me is that some people—and you all know who I mean—undercut you! I mean I have been very badly hurt by that. Let's face it, one guy wiped out a few people."

"You mean John?"

"Who do you think—of course!"

"That's right," said the quieter member of the group, "John has ruined planters; absolutely ruined them. I used to always count on being able to make something on my planters but he ruined that business." She looked at me, saw my puzzlement, and said: "He sells 'em for $3. What can you do? Three bucks! I can't make 'em anymore. I haven't made a planter for months."

"Exactly! And what's worse, his planters are awful—they're inferior, cheap. People who buy 'em blame all of us when the stuff is bad. I wish there was something we could do about it."

"Oh no," said the young one, "that's the whole thing I like about it—you can actually make your stuff and take it down to the Market and compete—hey!—that's what it's all about. Now you gotta do that; that's how it works. I think that's exciting, you can make it and then sell it."

"Oh sure, that sounds great," the older woman countered. "But here we are—all of us in competition with one another. You, me, everybody here. We work together and so on, but we're out to beat each other, too. And the thing is some people can come in here—we've seen them—and only spend a month or two learning and then go out and sell pots. And they are lousy pots! Look, I think that a teapot that is too heavy, impossible to lift when it's full, that won't pour, should be thrown out of the Saturday Market. That's what I think. Functional pots should be functional!"

"Sure, but who's going to decide?" asked the younger one. "I say the public decides—they should buy what's good and ignore what's bad. I love the idea that someone who's been making pots only six months can sell. That's a big plus for the system as far as I'm concerned. You can learn a craft, make something and sell it. Terrific!"

"Maybe, but I'd still like to see more standards."

The women said each paid $8 a month for a license for their booths at the Market, and 10 percent of proceeds went to the management. As they described it, if you had sold there 15 times you were supposed to get a reserved spot, but there were always more people than spaces so there had to be a lottery, a drawing to see who got the available spots. Then when oldtimers lost they objected loudly, saying there were too many potters now.

"Four years ago," said the older woman, "when we started out down there, it was very warm, very friendly. But now . . . ."

"Then how can a potter with a family make a steady living?" I asked.

"I don't know if he can," said the younger woman. "The ones I know who do are just real laid back, man, you know? They don't mind living in vans and selling in the street. They're getting by and they like the lifestyle. It's not bad . . . ."

"It depends on what you call making a living," said the quietest woman. "Actually, some people can make a whole lot of money doing some things, but they don't like it. So there's got to be more than money in it. As for me—I just like to make pots."

They agreed that they should be doing that very thing right now and went back to work. I walked up front to look at the sales room. There were some well-formed, professionally decorated and fired pieces. Overall, however, the quality of pots—there must have been 150 on display—ranged from poor to good. A few were possibly excellent, some hopeless. The quiet potter came by and said she had been trying porcelain for a year—"just enough to appreciate the kind of work that Coleman does. It is really exceptional. I don't want you to think from what was being said in there that we don't know that. Porcelain takes more time, more attention. It is simply more work, a lot more—I'm really struggling with it."

She reported doing fairly well financially, although her pots did not need to bring in major income; her husband was the family provider. She said a fair day for her at the Saturday Market would gross $150; a good day $200; and anything near $300 was considered great. She hoped to develop more sales outlets and once a year had a sale at her house.

The woman had shared a studio with another woman potter for quite a while but it was hard: "You can go crazy trying to avoid copying each other," she said. "It's so difficult to remember where you got an idea—from something you saw in a book, or dreamed, or maybe saw on your friend's wheel a month ago. That, plus problems over sharing space and clay and so on finally put an end to working together. I thought we would stay friends that way, but now I see her pots—with *my* forms! Ha! Potting can really put a strain on a friendship."

As I was preparing to leave the Potter's Workshop, the owner and manager, Jean Noe, arrived. Tall and extroverted, with a friendly and self-confident manner, Mrs. Noe said she and her husband had bought the workshop in early 1977 after moving to Oregon from the Midwest.

"I've always been in arts-and-crafts," she said, "love it. I was making batik and selling it at art fairs a couple of years ago, and was making probably $50 a day; but I kept seeing the potters making a lot—and I mean a *lot* more—so I decided to try pots. I did, and did fine. Then we got this place and it's going fine, too."

She said the numbers varied, but that the Workshop usually had about 15 renters who were full-time potters, 10 part-time; 15 professionals who rented only the firing facilities; and 30 students. The potters had many different goals, she said. About one-third had other jobs and pottery was merely a sideline. The rest were trying to make a significant part of their living from pottery.

"And, you know, they're doing it." Jean Noe said. "You can sell pots on many levels, many levels. It depends on how good you are, and how hard you want to work."

I mentioned visiting the Workshop's sales gallery, and Mrs. Noe agreed that the quality range was wide. But sales were very good, she said, partly because of the variety and also because the shop was exclusively for pottery; no other items were on display.

Before leaving, I phoned Ray Grimm at Portland State. He had forgotten our appointment, apologized, and invited me to his office.

I drove directly to the University, in the heart of the city, eager to meet Grimm. Coleman had told me, "Ray Grimm once made great pots—I mean *great* pots. They were a combination of smooth and rough like nothing I've ever seen. I'd sure like to get one of his old teapots, they were classics."

But no more—Grimm had not made important pots for several years, and Coleman said this apparently was because of poor health, aggravated by the gases, chemicals and dusts common to clay and kilns. He had turned his own artistic efforts mostly to sculpting and glass blowing, but continued to teach pottery at Portland State during a period in which many outstanding potters came through as students and teachers.

At the University, I quickly found the Art and Architecture building and Grimm, who was standing at his office door. After a brief introduction, he said, "You can wait in there and I'll be right back. Got to check the kiln."

I asked to come along; he said fine, and promptly took off at a fast clip with me at his heels.

"You know much about pots and kilns?" Grimm asked.

"Not so much," I said. "But a little. I can tell 'em apart . . . heh-heh."

"Oh, sure, yeah; that's fine—good. Com'on, we got this damned kiln—been giving the students a pain for a week so I said I'd come down today and watch it—my day off. It just won't get up to temperature, but I think I've got it figured out—we'll see. Hold on now, this'll take just a few minutes. . . ."

He moved briskly around the department, calling over to this student, conferring quietly with that one, checking here and there, upstairs and down. After about 15 minutes he said things looked pretty good and led me back to his office for the interview. He was obviously not looking forward to it, but said that as long as he had agreed to do it, "let's do it."

Grimm appeared to be about 60, with ruddy face, thinning silver-grey hair, thick eyeglasses, and a quick laugh that was not always amused. His speech was colorful and sometimes came in word bursts. The conversation was vigorous and interesting to me, but I never quite got rid of a feeling that I was keeping him from something, although he assured me this was not the case. Part of my feeling this way came from his restlessness, which sometimes made him seem about ready to dash off somewhere, and part from his suggestion that the book I was working on was not worth the trouble. He did not say this outright, but asked more than once if *I* thought it was worth it. Grimm apparently objected because of differences with Coleman in potting philosophy and taste, and because he seemed to believe that a book about *a* potter was a personal tribute merited by only the greatest masters.

I began by mentioning the stories of the big names in local pottery that had studied with him and/or taught at Portland State. Grimm nodded and said, "It was a great and exciting time for pottery around here. I had them all in my classes—Jerry Glynn, Wally Schwab, Bill Creitz, and so many others. Tom (Coleman) came later, of course, to teach; and I know his work. He's a beautiful craftsman and artist—I like him, like his work. Oh yes, it's very fine...but, ah, of course I must be honest here—my own particular taste is for work that is, ah, let's say *less precise*. Do you know what I mean? I would lean more toward the work of someone like Roland White—do you know him?" I said I did not and Grimm said, "His work is very similar to Coleman's but more spontaneous. They are going in their own directions, of course—Roland more emotional, and I guess I prefer that...if I had to choose."

Concerning the problems of a potter making a living, Grimm said he knew the difficulties from personal experience, and that teaching had been his answer. When he finished art studies in St. Louis he had realized the need for a financial base and debated whether to teach or to become a fireman, which with long shifts on and off left time for art. Grimm elected teaching and said it had worked out; he had not had to rely on selling his art to support his family.

I mentioned the Saturday Market for some reason and Grimm tensed and said sternly: "I *despise* the Saturday Market. Now I wouldn't have said that 10 years ago—not because I wouldn't have felt that way then, but because I didn't open my mouth so freely then. Nope, those guys at the Market sell their work for pennies, there's no respect. And you get such a lot of crap there—really bad pots alongside good ones. There are no standards, no standards at all—it is an awful place."

I observed that the Market did give potters a sales outlet, to which Grimm said that there were always outlets, and repeated that integrity and standards of craftsmanship were treated much too casually at the Market.

The discussion turned to why some artists succeeded with the public and others did not, and Grimm said: "The genius is the one that has the ability to put it together *and* to have it seen. In his way, Tom is doing that." Shortly after that, he said, "Slickness—what *I* call slickness—can take you places...maybe...up with the power and prestige people." I sensed he was making a point and asked if he was linking Tom and slickness with being seen and success and so forth. I did not catch Grimm's reply exactly but it sounded as if he said something like Coleman's "glamour boy" qualities had served him well among the high society set that bought artworks. When I asked if that was what he meant, Grimm looked at me, smiled meaningfully, and said, "Well, some say so."

A bit later, during lunch at a sandwich shop, Grimm said, "Coleman is making a living at art—and it seems that he is doing very well. I've always said that the main ingredient is determination. Really, sheer determination is what it takes. The talent is born in you, that must be there, though it may not always be obvious or apparent—and sometimes it is *so* hidden. Anyway, you must have determination if that talent is to come out, if you are to make something of it. . . ." He paused, then added, "Of course, the artist must also have something to say, must have a feeling about life—and he must struggle. And then, of course, he must have media and people—an audience—to look at his work. And he must challenge those viewers to wonder."

I asked whether he thought the ability to create wonder could be learned.

"You can have genius," Grimm said, "but if you can't execute it or show it, then it fails. And I don't believe that the artist knows when he does his best work; I don't. Things you think are great, are not. Oh God—how the stuff can play with your emotions. You know how hard you worked on something, you have struggled with it and sweated, and you have become *so* involved. But I'll tell you, in my case, if I hadn't finished what I didn't like, I would never have had shows. Nope, I never like my best things. Thank God I have a wife who is a good artist and speaks up. I argue bitterly sometimes about my stuff—whether this succeeds or that fails—and later I have to admit I was wrong." He laughed and continued, "It's very difficult to be an artist—even the production potter must hype himself up day after day. And so do I—I must hype myself up. And when I'm working on my sculpture it's a challenge; I talk to it and to myself and there's this pain in my belly—acute pain, *excruciating* pain—but when it's there I know the piece is going to work out. And if I don't go through all that, the work will fail. It's always that way."

I mentioned that Coleman had admired Grimm's pottery immensely and quoted Tom's praise of the teapots. Grimm seemed pleased and said, "Really, did he say that? Well, that's good to hear. Yes, I did make some pots in my time, I guess. And the teapots, yep, I always did have a special feeling about them. Glad to hear he feels that way."

Asked why he no longer made pots, Grimm shook his head slowly and said, "I had to quit—the doctor said the allergies were just too much—that. . .and I got tired."

As we talked about his potting days he became reflective. "You know," he said, "one of the great influences—perhaps the most important single influence on my work—was when I spent two weeks with Hamada. He was visiting the U.S., and had a workshop in Seattle—it was in the middle sixties sometime—and some of us went up. I tell you, it was something I'll never forget. Hamada had charisma, he left an impression that is still with me—and yet I have to wonder if he was like some other great people, ones who establish an aura of great humility but in reality may be quite the opposite. Whatever the case, Hamada influenced me; he had this aura of grandeur with humility. He opened the workshop and we just sat there. He threw lopsided pots, said nothing, and we just watched. This went on for a few hours, and he had a long row of pots. Then this potter we knew, came late, sat down with us, glanced at the rack full of pots and said: 'Funny—all students' pots look alike, don't they?' I'll never forget that," Grimm said, rocking with laughter. Then, serious again, he went on: "You know, Hamada never worked hard, just kept turning out the pots. But when he was done I looked at those pots—and they were live, *breathing* pots. He never struggled, just sat there and was surrounded by these pots." The wonderment was still in Grimm's voice a dozen years later.

"There was this Zen concept to everything," he said. "At the end Hamada broke one third of the pots; sold another third to the workshop students—very cheap; and sold the rest at his regular prices."

Grimm smiled and leaned back, stretching out his legs and seeming to sigh with his body.

About evaluating specific pots, he said, "It's hard to judge a piece of pottery sometimes; I may like something one day, not like it the next—but it is almost always the simple ones I like best. They don't sing out at first, but you get to liking them more and more as you look at them, and live with them...that's the thing about Hamada, he makes living pieces, really—they have the spontaneity of life."

When I showed him the slides of Coleman's pots, Grimm made few comments and afterwards said there were "no surprises. It was just about as I expected. Tom's an excellent craftsman and artist, as I said earlier—but, to be honest, as I also said before, it's not exactly my kind of pot."

When he had said that the first time I took it as simply an expression of a difference in approach and taste between Grimm and Coleman, but now he had repeated it and was going on—"Some say Tom's pots are cold; I don't know...maybe a little."

It would seem that this was a crucial point for someone who had just proclaimed his love for warm pots. After a pause, Grimm referred to a comment I had made during the slides about Coleman working hard on his red glaze and being pleased with it: "That red—hmmm," Grimm said. "You know, that's just for the artist's sake, to show he can do it. It's *not* attractive. No, I really don't like the red—*nobody* does like it much."

That, essentially, ended our conversation. It had lasted over two hours and I had wondered a few times if Grimm was putting me on. I simply could not tell. And now the statement about *nobody* liking the red glaze struck me as absurd—some people liked it; *I* liked it. The statement made me feel that Grimm was deeply annoyed, and telling me so. I felt he probably had been annoyed throughout our discussion, or even before it started. Perhaps it was my persistence or mundane questions, or Coleman. Maybe it was all of those things, and maybe there was something to do with a man who loved to make pots, and made great ones, but had to give it up, could not do it any more and watched others doing it, taught them, and now was being subjected to questioning—mostly about a young potter who worked differently than he did—by a stranger who had never been a potter, who couldn't know what it was like.

The day had enhanced my awareness of the complexity and competitiveness of the pottery world. I had been in touch with two different quarters of that world—the university where art was theoretically dominant, and the streetside workshop where we talked mostly about sales. In both places, though, people said they loved pots.

As often before, I had to wonder how much of what I heard and saw carried nuances and subtleties only a potter could appreciate. I was learning, but as an observer—pottery was not my life, my bread and butter, or my obsession. I was also learning, though, how it was all those things . . . and mud-pies for many different people.

The long meeting with Grimm heightened some doubts I had about my perceptiveness and my ability to come to terms with potters and pottery. I wanted more opinions, more feedback on things in general and on Coleman's work in particular.

I arranged to show slides of Tom's most recent pots to Judy Teufel, a well-regarded professional potter and teacher who said teaching gave her rewards as great as potting. In both endeavors, Judy believed the doing was as important as the results—getting there was a major part of the fun.

She was firing a salt-glaze kiln at her farm this particular weekend, joined by Walt Gordinier and Louise Neilson. Walt had been concentrating lately on large handbuilt pieces and had just produced a one-man show of terra-cotta boxes. Louise, a non-professional, had been making pots about five years and was a serious and skilled potter. After they finished loading the kiln late in the evening, I showed the slides and asked for opinions based not only on the photos but also on Coleman's previous work.

All three said the new pieces were spectacular, the shapes and colors excellent. Two cited the red glazes as particularly outstanding. Judy said she had long been impressed by Coleman's technique in handling porcelain and in decorating; she liked many of his pots and nearly bought one in his last Portland show—"it's fine work, no question of that...but it's just not my style."

Judy's own pottery was earthier, and she made a point of not overworking a form or decoration, seeking a moderately controlled interaction of elements with a focus on spontaneity; she valued naturalness over refinement. "There is just too much control for me in Tom's pots," Judy said. "They just aren't me—but that's a difference in taste not a criticism." She laughed a little and added: "For me, such perfection is like watching the Russian ice-skating couple in the last Winter Olympics—remember them on TV? Oh, what precision...flawless technique...so perfect, so exactly right that you wanted to see him skate across her hair!—to do something, *anything*, to break that perfection, to be more human—to stumble, to blow it somehow."

"Oh no," Gordinier said at once. "I don't feel that way at all. I really responded to these pieces. I can appreciate the intensity with which he was working, and I think I understand that one-to-one challenge of the potter and material. I can really feel those things in his work—the competition, the drive to control the clay. To me it's exciting."

Walt added, "I also like the purity of his forms—I definitely do—and his lines, his use of space, and interior space, too. Of course, it's like Judy says, a certain amount of it is taste, but I am really impressed. I like it!"

I was delighted that such experienced and accomplished potters could make such different appraisals.

Louise had to leave right after the slides ended and I telephoned her later. She said Coleman's new pots were excellent and that she had always been impressed by his work: "The first time I saw a show of his pots I was literally stunned, I couldn't believe it. It was as if some ancient Chinese master had been reincarnated; really. I think his work is incredible—far and above anybody else's that I've seen in porcelain. It's off the charts."

I also telephoned Gerry Williams, the editor of *Studio Potter* in Manchester, New Hampshire. Williams had visited Coleman while touring the Pacific Northwest. In answer to my questions, Williams said he rated the region's pottery "quite high" and Tom Coleman as "a very good potter, but, of course, like all of us, he still has a way to go."

Pressed to say more, Williams added that Coleman's work was "facile, a trifle overworked, and a bit flamboyant. Of course, this is due to his exuberance and vitality. After Tom has traveled some more and seen more work, I believe this will be adjusted. I have very good feelings about Tom's work and future."

The next issue of Williams' magazine, Winter 1977-78, led off with an article about 15 Oregon potters with a page on Coleman, describing him as a "widely respected master." It was the only time "master" was used in the 17-page story.

On the evening of November 2, Tom and I attended the opening of a show by Bill Creitz at the Portland Arts & Crafts School gallery. After looking at the pots we spent nearly two hours with Bill and other potters, talking and helping empty and re-empty the punch bowl. The gossip and hassling was intriguing, and after the gallery closed a group convened at a potters' hangout. The banter continued and with each pitcher of beer the jesting gained in directness what it lost in wit. However, there was only one significant comment I remembered the next day. I overheard it as Coleman was deep in conversation with a burly, red-bearded Scotsman introduced as Brian Johnstone, who worked out of the Potters' Workshop. I was still trying to recall what was in my head about a Brian at the Workshop when his words to Coleman came through foam-flecked whiskers: "My God, mon," Brian said, "yuv gaw ta loosen oop. Yuhrr pawts are just too tight!"

THE ART AND THE ENDS

The Colemans' Seattle show was extended a week because of its popularity, Ruth said, and now would close November 13. Tom would drive up that day to fetch the unsold pots and I would go along to make a few more photographs. In view of the extension, I expected that many more pots had been sold, but the Colemans had no fresh news about sales.

We started early on the 13th and talked most of the way. Tom recalled the previous trip, how much he had enjoyed parts of it but what a letdown he had later—"Oh boy, I really had a downer—miserable. Hit me hard. Hung on a long time, too; but I eventually got over it. Been working pretty good lately."

Asked how he regarded his work for the show now that time had elapsed, he said he was still convinced it was the best show he had ever done. As for the lukewarm response at the opening—"What can you do? Who knows what people are going to like. I think it was my best and I can't worry about it. Sure could use some bucks, though."

To try and improve business he had been considering opening a shop with the aid of his mother and step-father, featuring the work of the Colemans and three or four more potters—"everybody seems serious, but it's just talk so far."

He also mentioned working on some softer, duller finishes on his porcelain—"I've been considering that for quite a while and now seems like a good time to do it. Actually, though, what I'd really like to do is get away, take a break—stop making pots and travel. But, of course, that's out—even if we could afford it—you just can't go away for six months. You'd come back and find, just like Horsley says, you lost your slot! So many young potters are waiting to sell for peanuts. You can't blame them, but you get upset that the public doesn't know or demand better quality."

Coleman had been working in stoneware since the show and spent all of one day and night mixing 10 tons of clay with Tom Tibbs in Tibbs' brother-in-law's factory. It was exhausting, Coleman said, and the worst part was all the clay and chemical dust that got into your respiratory system. "Hazards of making pottery, no way to avoid 'em," he said.

We reached Seattle about noon and went straight to the Northwest Craft Center. A brief look around the gallery disclosed that some more pots had red "sold" stickers, but many did not. Then, while Tom talked in the office with Ruth Namura, I chatted with a woman attending the main sales area and realized she was the one in a kimono-like dress I had seen admiring Tom's red teapot. I assumed she had bought it, but she said, "somebody else got it. I'm sorry, I should have; I waited too long to decide."

Tom was among her favorite potters and "one of the most important around the Northwest—if not *the* most important," she said in a hushed voice, apparently so that he would not overhear. "And I'm not the only one who thinks so," she assured me—"Oh my, so many potters and students came to see this show; they just loved it."

We went to work (Tom was packing up the pots of the Tibbses as well as his own; they were on a trip) and Ruth stopped by the showroom from time to time. I asked her opinion of Coleman's current pots compared with previous ones, which I had never seen.

"I'd say that this show was good, very good," Ruth said. "Actually, it was the best I've ever had."

She said this so casually that I thought she must have meant "one of the best" or the best of Coleman's. Ruth had managed the gallery since it opened in 1963, and had consistently shown the top potters of a wide area ranging from Northern California to British Columbia and inland to Idaho and Montana. I asked if she meant the show was one of the best or Coleman's best.

Ruth shook her head: "No," she said, "it was *the* best. Simply the best—ever."

Best in sales? I asked.

"Oh my, no," she said. "We've had much, much better sales; but this was the best show."

What made it the best?

"The quality of the pots to start with . . . and the variety . . . and also the fact that lots of potters came, lots of people who *really know* pots, and they were *so* interested—fascinated! Really—my best show ever."

I wanted to pursue this, but frequent interruptions prevented a sustained conversation. Over the afternoon, however, I was able to get more details. Other factors in her appraisal were the overall quality of Coleman's craftsmanship, imagination and ideas, plus the refinement and idealism evident in the pots.

"I've seen a lot of fine potters—a lot," Ruth said, "and Tom, like the best of them, has something so decent, so straight and sincere about his work and about himself, that it comes through in the pots."

She added that among the many potters who came to the exhibit it was common to hear remarks like, "it's too much". . . ."awesome". . . "beyond me". . . ."I could never do it. . . ."

I asked if that was unusual for a show.

"So many is unusual," she replied, "but, of course, over the years I've heard it like that now and then about all the big names."

This brought to mind the stories of potters who reached the top and could not stay because they burned themselves out. I asked Ruth if she believed this was a common problem.

"No, the few great ones stay up there. Most of the others simply couldn't, or wouldn't stay . . . . I think, though, that maybe Tom will. He's capable of it."

We worked late, finishing well after the gallery's 8 p.m. closing. Ruth took us to a Chinese restaurant where, between several excellent courses of food, we talked pots and potters. It was 2 a.m. by the time we started back to Portland so we found a motel, slept fitfully on lumpy beds, and were on the road again about seven o'clock in the morning. Conversation sputtered along, but after coffee and doughnuts at a roadside shop it became passably coherent.

Tom seemed amazed to hear the details of Ruth's judgment of his show as her best ever. "I can hardly believe that," he said. "Of course I love to hear it, but. . . *that* is far out—never heard her say something like that before. Maybe she's just putting you on . . . ."

I did not think so. All of her comments had supported the idea and we discussed it several times. I told Tom this and asked if they had done any computation of sales. He said no, nothing was very exact—"but never mind sales, who cares"—they had done fairly well, he guessed, and so had the Tibbses.

In fact, it appeared that approximately 29 or 30 of the Colemans' original 96 pots were spoken for. These were valued at between $3,000 and $3,500. Expenses would run more than $2,000.

It was not a great return on nearly three months' work by two people. So, as we drove along, the back of the old station wagon was three-fourths filled with pots. Some would sell later, of course, but still. . . .

Less than halfway home it threatened to rain and the leaden sky seemed to dull our spirits; we were tired anyway. Talk died out and my thoughts wandered.

In the next hours and in subsequent weeks I went back often over the time I had spent trying to document Coleman's work and learn about pot-making. I dwelt on the hours working in the studio and talking on the porch, and recalled the people I had met—from Elaine, who was a strong factor in Tom's work, and an impressive potter in her own right; to Susanna Kuo, who had played a significant role in Tom's recent work; and to my meetings with all the others, each one of whom added measurably to my knowledge.

Coleman, of course, was at the forefront. Surprisingly, though the image was no longer dominant, it was still possible to recall flashes of the Golden Boy spinning up pots with ease and living the good life with his beautiful family in the countryside. Coleman was responsible for this image, not just because of his looks and manner, but also because he could make the work look so easy. He served as the perfect example for the cliche about lucky folks who earn their living doing work they enjoy: "Imagine, doing what you love to do and getting paid for it? What could be better than that?"

I knew now that Coleman labored long hours, days on end, despite broiling heat, asthma attacks, allergies, and backaches; that he sometimes spent two hours on the wheel with a single pot, improving it by fractions, insisting it reach its limits—while the potter reached his, too. And he had done this for more than a decade.

For what—big money? Glowing reviews? Success, fame, screaming fans? Perhaps such things tickled his imagination, but they were outside the potters' realm.

Clearly, Coleman was doing it because he wanted to. There were other jobs, but he *wanted* to make pots and paint on them. And no matter how difficult potting was, the cliche was right: it *is* a great thing to make a living doing what you love to do. And Coleman was doing it.

I had seen him in a concentrated flow of work, occasionally accelerating into passionate bursts, and continually seeking to grow, to discover where his skills and intuition and training could take him. And it had been done within the context of a family and making a living, of trying to make art and ends meet.

For years he had moved increasingly onto his own path. Idols of the past had faded, their influence lingering but no longer directing his efforts.

At times I felt that Coleman represented an intense doing and searching within set boundaries. At his most creative he was struggling without the aid of a map. It was demanding and exhilarating, miserable and joyful—and drudgery.

And again the question came—for what? Simply wanting to was somehow not enough.

Of course there was no simple answer. In practical terms, Coleman was merely trying to keep going with one foot in the world of art and the other in the workaday-raise-a-family world. Sometimes those worlds complemented one another, but often they did not. Hence the super frustration and confusion over being—or trying to be—a serious artist in the super-industrial, super-material, super-fast 1970s U.S.A. It does not seem the most appealing climate for "art"; at least not the kind rooted in the classic forms and colors of anonymous Chinese masters more than a thousand years old.

So Coleman has had to play multiple roles. Everybody does to varying degrees, but a self-employed craftsman/artist working at home experiences moment-to-moment kaleidoscopic role changes: children in the studio—is he Coleman the potter or father? Wife working alongside—is he colleague, teacher, or husband? Bills to be paid—is he artist or breadwinner? And with inflation being what it is, the last role was never far offstage—artwork being among the first items crossed off the budget when finances tighten. Then Coleman the production potter turned out more casseroles and platters, mugs and tumblers, and was thankful for them.

On a more abstract level, Coleman played additional roles in matching his compulsion to make pottery with his compulsion for family, love, identity, and home; for having the kind of place for his children that he did not have.

Here was the true-grit struggle—striving to make art and a family; falling short on both sides too often, but continuing to try for both. And there Coleman had kept the dilemma more-or-less at bay. This had not been a do-or-die romantic answer, not uncompromising idealism—it had been an answer that life seemed to allow those who try just hard enough to eat their cake and have it. But, of course, if they got too greedy they could lose both—and what was left of their sanity, too.

Coleman, then, had lived a dual professional life to match his dilemma. He had the production pots to relax with, to crank out, and make sure money; and he had the porcelain art pieces to struggle and grow with and perhaps make some money.

In these endeavors Coleman served as a reminder that talent is vital but still needs strong doses of determination, perseverance, and hard work. (Coleman also provided a reminder that the right wife may be as important as any of those.) A Portland gallery manager told me that Coleman was the only one of the many potters she saw who came in regularly to look over his pieces, weed them out, and seek opinions from anyone who was serious and had thought about pots. "He is constantly trying to grow," she said, "and already he can hold his own with any potter in the country."

As for potting countrywide, I was fascinated to learn that so many persons were making money from pots and that the markets were so uneven. Following a boom period in the late 1960s and early '70s, Pacific Northwest potters—many Oregonians anyway—had been complaining lately that it was so competitive that making a living was very tough. But in Indiana, production potter Richard Peeler said (in *Ceramics Monthly*, April 1978) that the market for handmade pots was "great—unbelievable! . . . We feel it is relatively easy to make a living from one's own production of pottery today. I cringe when I hear potters describe their incomes as 'modest' or 'meager.' Given today's market, no one needs to settle for a meager income unless he wants to."

Perhaps the answer was to go to Indiana or redefine meager and modest.

And what about pottery as "art?" I realize it has traditionally been on the fringe of the classic fine arts such as painting and sculpture, but it would seem to be accepted nowadays in most circles. But how many potters make their way strictly as artists? Few at best. But before getting too upset on behalf of art potters, it may be worth asking how many poets make a living strictly as poets? Or playwrights as playwrights? John Updike says that "hardly a hundred American men and women earn their living by writing, not counting journalists and suppliers of scripts to the media." Obviously these latter groups are the production potters of the word business.

The complaint is heard in each of these fields that high-quality work is too often overlooked by the public in favor of inferior quality—another cliche that seems certain of long life.

These matters raise questions about how we as individuals and as a people feel about the creation of art for its own sake. Should there be more subsidization of artists? Should we look to European practices? Or simply let the marketplace make the decisions? It is more complex than I am prepared to deal with, but it does seem to me that the Colemans of the world touch the heart of the issue. They are not ones to go wading through the red tape and bureaucratic sorting out, the salesmanship and persistence they say are commonly associated with grants, awards, and various assistance programs for artists. Nor, usually, do they excel at business (i.e., Coleman's handling of the show flyer. He later agreed that he should have done something to assure the flyer's early completion but just could not get excited about such things when he was making pots.).

I imagine that freed from everyday worries over making a living that Tom Coleman would produce extraordinary pottery. With luck, he will anyway. And who knows how much his achievements have been influenced—improved?—by being under economic pressures; he has talked of having masochistic tendencies and claimed that one of the main reasons he liked porcelain was that it gave him so many problems.

And so Coleman will surely continue on his way. His work thus far has occasionally been too varied, overworked, overdone. He has sometimes made too many pots and decorated them too much. And in the face of this, some critics insist he has been too rigid and tightly disciplined.

But whatever the words and judgments, it has all been—is—part of the learning and the search. His pots have a vigor and delight that reflect a pleasure and joy and excitement about life, despite all of its ups and downs. And presuming the downs are not too severe, as they have not been thus far, the years ahead should grant Coleman the maturity and wisdom to fulfill the promise of his past accomplishments.

In achieving that, I have wondered if the optimistic faith of Michael Cardew will apply. Cardew has said: "The essential thing is that the potter does not merely follow what his public wants but leads it, so that in the end they want what he wants. He will often have to wait a long time before he is accepted. He makes life hard for himself at first, but later on his public will come to him because in his workshop the potter's art is alive."

It is a hopeful idea, and pottery's utilitarian qualities favor it in some ways, but I wonder about other aspects. There is something so traditional and conservative about much pottery—perhaps it is inherent in the strict limits of materials and the rigid disciplines required—that the innovative artist faces serious problems. Perhaps that's why pottingdom lacks names known in every household—the Rembrandts and Picassos and Calders. The potters known best to laymen are Wedgewood and the anonymous Chinese masters of 1,000 years ago; asked to name a living potter, most would likely name their Aunt Maxine, who took a course at the neighborhood hobby shop and made quite a nice ashtray.

But in that, too, there may be hope.

So it was November 14, 1977—fourteen weeks to the day since Coleman had begun working on the show—and we were nearing the end of our return drive from Seattle. I asked Tom what he planned to do next.

"I'm not sure," he said. "We've been making pots for Christmas—to sell and for our own gifts—and we've got to take more pots to Contemporary Crafts. . . . We've also been invited to enter a group show at Marylhurst College and have to send slides to a competition in Los Angeles . . . and we have a big show at the Whitebird (gallery) next summer. So we've got plenty to keep us busy. Guess we'll just keep going. Who knows, we still might take a trip somewhere."

I asked for more details about his idea to soften the finish on his porcelain.

"I've been thinking quite a bit," Tom said. "I've spent the last three years trying to achieve as much control as possible over my tools and material, and now it's time to start loosening up. I can't tell you what I'm going to do next; I don't know. But I do recognize some changes in my work and I know more are coming."

Pressed for more on this, he said, "I really don't know what it will be. Actually, I dislike talking about that sort of thing—it's impossible; I've tried, but I just haven't found the words. If I knew where I was going, I'd be there. And talking about it is inadequate."

I thought, hoped at least, that I was beginning to understand; no matter what kinds of pots he made, some would arouse feelings, ask questions, make statements that no words could do. It was time, then, to be quiet—to let the pots speak. Surely that was the way to learn from them, about them, and about Thomas Coleman and his kind of mud-pies.

This begins a presentation of photographs in the sequence the pottery was made—from throwing to decorating and firing, and ending with color plates of the finished work. All of the pottery is porcelain and was produced in the Colemans' Canby studio for exhibition in Seattle, October-November, 1977, with the exception of a few pieces in the color pages which were made shortly afterward. Color photos marked by an asterisk are of pots made by Elaine Coleman.

Tom Coleman leans back for a better perspective of a two-section, 2½-foot-high vase he is throwing.

In the main workroom of the Colemans' studio, Tom is at the wheel, large pieces await trimming and bisque firing.

Coleman uses a rib to finish a piece, left, then studies it, and places it beside a companion pot to dry. The 103-degree heat of the afternoon speeded drying and seemed to heighten the porcelain's natural glow.

Multiple exposures of Coleman throwing a vase show the clay rising in a series of hand pulls starting with the opening of the pot, above. The last two pictures illustrate the diminishing increases achieved as the clay approaches its limits. Other views of the same pot and procedures are on the next two pages.

Coleman's hand descends into the vase to begin an upward pull.

The finished vase stands still on the wheel.

Elaine Coleman builds a double-walled box.

Using a dentist's tool, Elaine carves a decoration on the lid of a tall box.

Throwing of a large two-section jar begins, top, with the upper section being placed upon the lower one. Then, having scored the exterior seam joining the sections, Coleman works on the interior.

Lifting clay from the thicker base section to the upper portion, Coleman improves the jar's general form and mouth.

Having achieved the basic form, Coleman refines it to achieve the desired shape drawn on the blackboard. Pot stands about three feet high.

Ribs help finish the form and remove throwing lines to provide the surface smoothness Coleman wants to paint upon.

After final work on the mouth and the addition of encircling lines for decoration, more than an hour of sustained work shows in Coleman's face.

The pot stands finished, except for the lid, as Tom takes a phone call. Days later, upon opening the bisque kiln, he found the jar had cracked in firing.

Coleman uses calipers to measure the portion of a sectional vase that will be joined to a similar piece on another wheel. Working the joined sections, he becomes unhappy with the upper part, trims the mouth, finishes the piece and carries it away.

Coleman works on the mouth, and later puts the completed vase among a variety of drying porcelains.

A pinched foot is attached to the bottom of a bowl; a curl of leather-hard clay is trimmed from the lid of a yo-yo jar.

Yo-yo bowls fill the shelf of a drying rack.

Pots, some decorated and others awaiting decoration, fill a table as Coleman uses his throwing wheel as an easel and paints with oxides on a tall jar.

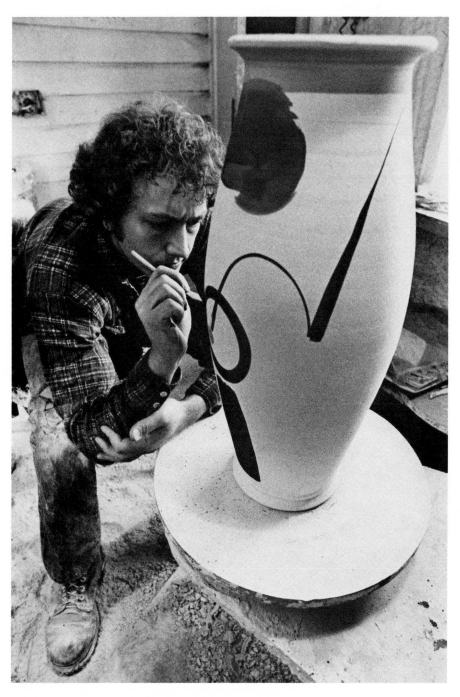

Carefully bracing his hand, Coleman concentrates on the final strokes of the jar's abstract decoration.

Coleman mimes the first strokes, then paints an unorthodox teapot with abstract circles, dots, and lines.

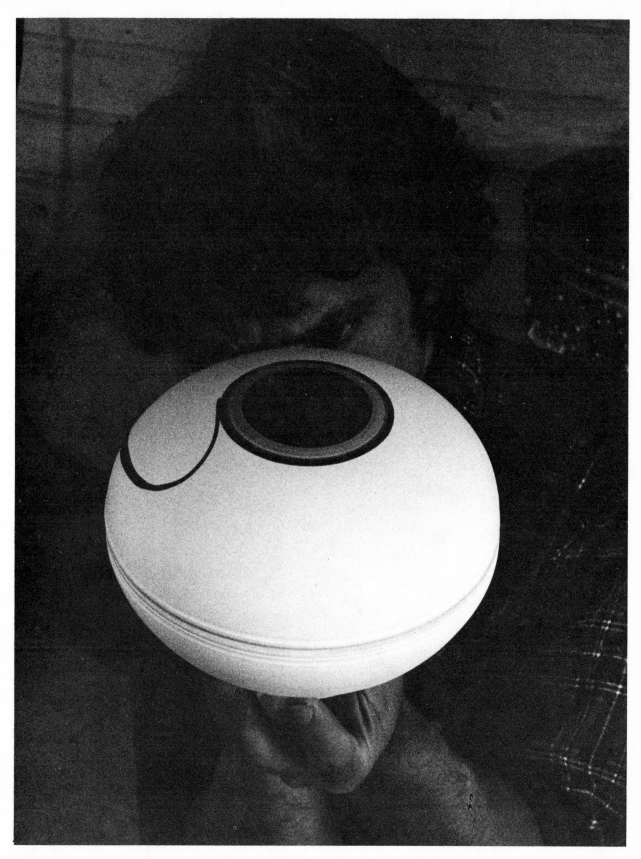

Coleman decorates a covered bowl.

Coleman decorates, clockwise, a large jar with Queen Anne's lace; another jar with cherries; a pot while using a weed as a model. A table holds ready-to-fire pots. Elaine watches Tom finish a design.

Decorated 2½-foot-high jars and other pieces await the final firing.

Coleman carries a tall bottle to the cart-on-rails that will roll into the kiln. He studies the narrow clearance between pots and the ceiling of the 75-cubic-foot Minnesota flat top kiln.

Pots are fitted carefully onto the kiln cart's shelves. Coleman takes a final look from inside the kiln before rolling in the pots.

Flames spurt as Coleman pulls a kiln brick to check cones. After firing, he peers anxiously at cooling pots.

He looks over rack filled with just-fired pots and then inspects each piece individually.

In Seattle, Tom ponders a problem in setting up the pottery exhibit before the opening night, center; three of the pots on display.

Teapot, copper red, 6″ high, 9″ wide with spout.

Ginger jar, copper red, 14½″ high, 8″ wide.

Platter, celadon with copper blush, 15″ across, 2″ high.

Narrow-necked bottle, copper red, 9″ high, 8½″ wide.

Oxide decorated forms: Top, covered jar approximately 27″ high, 22″ wide before firing; others, after firing, clockwise, lidded jar 12″ high, 12″ wide; bowl 5½″ high, 6½″ wide; platter 15″ across, 2½″ high; covered jar 22″ high, 18″ wide.

Tom Coleman inspects pots from a just-opened kiln.

Covered jar with ash-salt glaze, 12″ high, 11″ wide.

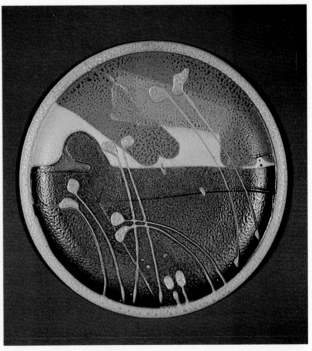

Platter with ash-salt glaze over white slip, 17½ " across, 2½ " high.

Platter with ash-salt glaze over colored slips, 12" across, 3" high.

Woven basket* with ash-salt glaze, 9" high, 6" wide.

Basket form with ash-salt glaze, 16" high, 10" wide.

Bevelled cylinder with ash-salt glaze, 9" high, 5" wide.

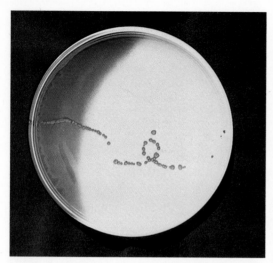

Platter with copper blush and copper wire line, 17″ across, 2½″ high.

Bowl with copper red inside and oxide decoration, 5½″ high, 6″ wide.

Cylinder with oxide and wax resist decoration, 18″ high, 8″ wide.

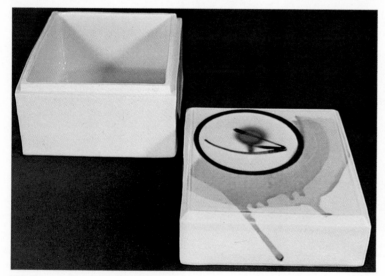

Slab box* with oxide decoration, 5½″ high, 7″ wide, 8″ long.

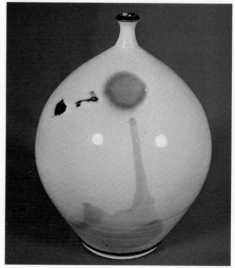

Bottle with oxide decoration, 8″ high, 5″ wide.

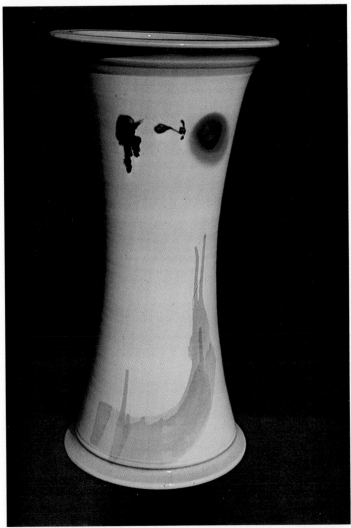

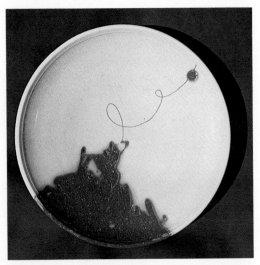

Platter with sifted ash over chun white glaze, 17″ across, 2½″ high.

Fluted vase with oxide decoration and celadon lip, 22″ high, 9″ wide.

Teapot with oxide decoration, 8½″ high, 9″ wide with spout.

Slab box*, 2½″ high, 4″ long.

Covered jar with oxide decoration, 10½″ high, 13″ wide.

Fluted vase with oxide decoration, 15″ high, 7″ wide.

Covered bowl with oxide decoration, 7½″ high, 10½″ wide.

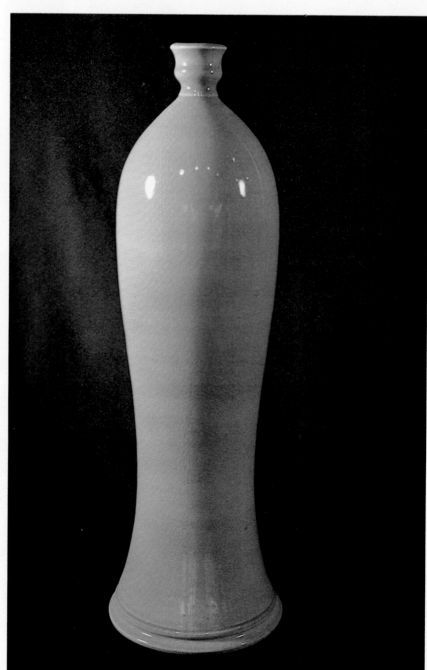

Bottle, celadon, 23″ high, 7″ wide.

Covered jar with oxide decoration, 25″ high, 9½″ wide.

Covered bowl, celadon, incised decoration, 4¼″ high, 6″ wide.

Small-necked bottle with oxide decoration, 9½″ high, 9″ wide.

Bowl, top, with celadon interior and oxide decoration, 5½″ high, 6½″ wide.
Slab box*, celadon, 4″ high, 3″ wide, 4½″ long.

Ginger jar, celadon, with incised decoration, 14″ high, 9″ wide.

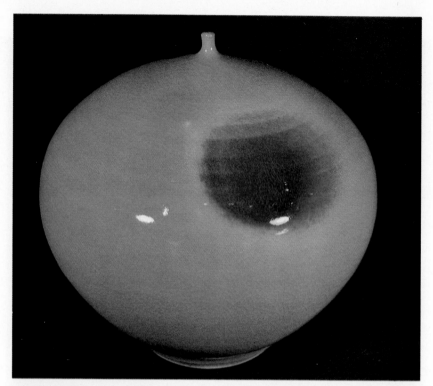

Small-necked bottle, celadon with copper blush, 8½″ high, 8″ wide.

Plate, celadon with incised decoration, 12″ across, 1½″ high.

Covered bowl, celadon with incised decoration, 4″ high, 4½″ wide.

Teapot, light celadon, 9″ high, 9″ wide, with spout.

Teapot, celadon, 11½″ high, 11½″ wide with spout.

Covered bowl with ash-salt glaze over black slip, 6½″ high, 9″ wide.

Teapot with ash-salt glaze, 9½″ high, 8″ wide with spout.

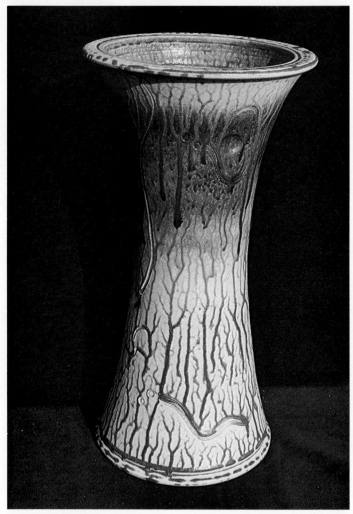

Fluted vase with ash-salt glaze, 19½″ high, 10″ wide.